BATTLE FOR THE TRUTH

SECOND EDITION

CREATION VERSUS EVOLUTION

H.D. CHIOU

ISBN: 978-1-969865-75-6 (sc)
ISBN: 978-1-969865-76-3 (e)

Rev. date: 06/01/2026

Preface

Throughout the past twenty-seven years, when I tried to evangelize into Christianity those people with engineering or scientific backgrounds, the major challenge has always been how to help them believe there is a loving God who created the universe and everything in it for humans to have an abundant life. The main difficulty has been that their education causes them to believe that the theory of evolution is the truth, and that science can explain everything in the universe. The theory of evolution emphasizes random mutations and natural selection; the point of life is then aimless, for life was formed by chance, excluding the God of creation. The theory of evolution, therefore, became the theoretical basis for atheism. This theory has spread and now deeply affects every aspect of human society. I have written five books in Chinese about science and Christianity to confront this atheistic worldview.

This second edition book you are holding in your hands can be regarded as the improved version of the first edition. The first edition was the English version of my fourth Chinese book, of the same title. This book has had significant modifications from the Chinese version, and I have added a second appendix, which discusses the signs of the cross hidden in Israel's Tabernacle and camping formation to support the existence of God and His salvation.

The purpose of this book is to prove that the creation account as told in the Bible is truth, based on recent scientific findings, and that the theory of evolution is not complete truth. Due to our limited human viewpoints, Darwin's studies had their limitations, which led to the following mistakes:

Darwin thought the structure of cells was very simple, and therefore the formation of the first "life" would have been easy. Without this first point of life, there would have been no starting point for evolution.

Darwin only observed micro-evolution (the God-given ability of species to adapt to their environments), and that only in small animals. He extended his theory to macro-evolution (evolution between species) without any scientific basis for this extrapolation.

This book introduces recent scientific findings, such as the structure of DNA and the complexity of the cell structure, to demonstrate that the theory of intelligent design makes far more sense than the theory of evolution, at the same time proving the biblical account of God's creation of the universe is true

This book emphasizes that God's creation was based on His love for human beings and that everything He created was made with that purpose in mind: to bless people. God created human beings with special care in His own image, and He gave them His Spirit to enable them to live with Him forever.

Acknowledgments

I would like to thank F. Scott Davis for editing the manuscript before its submission to Trilogy Publishers; Dr. Luke Huang, who supplied information about childbirth defects and human and ape hematology; my daughter, Faye Chiou, who helped me to modify some of the English content; and Ying Chen, Ph.D., for help in editing the initial Chinese work.

Finally, I would like to acknowledge the love and constant support of my wife, Fan Mei, throughout the fifty-seven years of our marriage.

Contents

Introduction

This book explores, from both scientific and biblical perspectives, whether the creation described in the Bible or the theory of evolution taught in biology classes is true. This is a complex question. People may believe in God and evolution, or they may not believe in God but believe in evolution. Two modern theories complicate this issue: the evolution theory and the Big Bang theory. This book mainly discusses the truth or falsity of these two theories.

What is "the truth"?[1] This is a question to which many people want to know the true answer. In this world, there are "truths" and then there are "false truths." This book will discuss which is *truth*: the God's creation or the theory of evolution.

The seeking of the Truth by ancient Philosophers

Throughout human history, many philosophers have sought the truth[1] about the origin or creation of the universe. In Chinese history, for example, Lao Tzu[2] called this truth "Tao." In the first chapter of the *Tao-Te Ching*[3] as translated by Lîm Gí-tông[4] it states:

"The Tao that can be told is not the Absolute Tao; The name that can be given is not the Absolute name. The Nameless is the origin of Heaven and Earth; The Named is the Mother of All Things."

What Lao Tzu said was that if he could talk about "Tao", then the "Tao" is not the *Absolute Tao*; if he can name the name, then the name is not the *Absolute name*. "Nothing" was the beginning of heaven and earth; "have" is the mother of all things.

In the summary of this passage: Lao Tzu knew there was a creator of the universe, but he felt that the creator is so great, he could not name Him.

In chapter 25 of the *Tao-Te Ching*, he states:

"Before the Heaven and Earth existed, There was something nebulous: Silent, isolated, Standing alone, changing not, Eternally revolving without fail, Worthy to be the Mother of All Things. I do not know its name And address it as Tao. If forced to give it a name, I shall call it "Great Being,

great implies reaching out in space, reaching out in space implies far-reaching, Far-reaching implies reversion to the original point."

The above statements told us that Lao Tzu felt the greatness of "Tao" and expressed His omnipresent. Lao Tzu called the truth that created the universe as "Tao". This "Tao" points directly to God. In the Gospel of John in the Chinese translated bible: "I*n the beginning there was "Tao" (the Word, in the English translated bible), the "Tao" was with God, and the "Tao" was God"* (John 1:1 KJV).

Ancient Greek philosophers are also pursuing the truth of all things in the universe. They thought about *"Where the universe came from?"* and *"What is the universe made of?"* They put forward many interesting theories in the process of thinking. British Bible scholar pastor David Pawson (1930 -2020)[5] pointed out that a philosopher named Heraclitus (B.C. 535-475 B.C.) was observing the ever-changing world around him. As he did so, a question was raised, that is, *why do all the phenomena occur in the world?* Heraclitus created Greek word (λόγος, Logos) to represent the answer to the question. The philosophical meaning of this word (Logos) is similar to Lao Tzu's "Tao". Pastor Pawson explained that the "Logos" in ancient Greece means the theory of studying a certain subject. For example, the "Logos" of studying organisms is biology. Others, such as physics, etc., are the "Logos" of a certain subject[6] All these subjects of study are just some of the partial principles that have been discovered in the universe. The "truth" discussed in this book is an universal truth that will never change, that is, the ultimate truth.

The religion's pursuit of the One True God

In terms of religion, people search for the one true God through the creatures in the universe. The apostle Paul told us: "*For since the creation of the world God's invisible qualities—his eternal power and divine nature—have been clearly seen, being understood from what has been made, so that people are without excuse*" (Romans 1:20 NIV). But without additional revelation from God, people could not find the one true God, because *"God is a Spirit"* (John 4:24 KJV), and man cannot see God. So, the ancient people were seeking God like "the blind men and the elephant." For that reason, there are many religions that have been created by humans,[7] worshiping all kinds of creatures as gods.

Ancient Greece had many gods, and their religion was filled with myths and stories of gods or goddesses who manipulated everything that took place on the earth. The Bible records that when the apostle Paul was in Athens, the city was full of idols, but there was also an altar with this inscription: *"TO*

AN UNKNOWN GOD". (Acts 17:16-23 kJV). From this we know that they believed in many gods

The people of ancient Mesopotamia also worshiped many gods. Babylonian culture believed that the universe was filled with gods. Every city, every clan, and every family had its own god. The size of the god depended on the degree of success of the people who worshiped him or her. (Many places in Taiwan still worship the god of each particular city.) The Bible tells us that Jehovah chose Abram (who was later renamed by God as Abraham) to leave the polytheistic environment in which he lived. God wanted Abraham to only worship Him. God led Abram from Ur in Mesopotamia to Harran and then to Canaan (Genesis 11:29–12:4; Acts 7:2–4). this is because Mesopotamia was a place filled with idols.

The ancient Egyptians revered the sun as the supreme god, while also viewing the Nile River and various animals as separate gods. The Bible tells us that the Ten Plagues God inflicted on the Egyptians (see Exodus 7-10) were directed against these false gods. Jehovah was demonstrating to the Egyptians that their false gods were of no use to them. Only Jehovah is the one true God. Jehovah's name would be glorified throughout the earth.

Ancient Chinese Confucianism respected the heavens and the earth, and its practitioners sacrificed to ghosts and gods. For example, Confucius said, "*How can you know about death before you figure out the purpose of living?*" Confucius did not believe it was possible for people to understand the world of ghosts and gods, nor was it possible to understand how gods controlled the natural world. The ancient Chinese even worshiped heaven itself as a god. Later, with the rise of Confucianism and Taoism, coupled with the introduction of Buddhism, everything was worshiped as part of the presence of the supernatural. In the past, Chinese emperors set up temples for loyal officials and worshiped them. People also built temples to honor the great men or women who died before them.

In Taiwan, the god of heaven, the god of land, the god of wealth, the god of the stove, the god of thunder, the god of the township, etc., are still worshiped. There are also many other strange religions in that country. Many "false gods" in which the people of Taiwan believe are evil spirits. Testimonies about the physical, mental, and family damage caused by believing in these "false gods," as well as the peace and blessings obtained after the people converting to belief in Jesus Christ, can be seen in many cases on *Good News TV* in Taiwan.

Hinduism believes that the material world is just an extension of the world of the gods. They believe that all animals are gods. They do not believe there is a creator, and they see the material world as indistinguishable from the spiritual world. Buddhism also believes there is no god. The leader of

Buddhism, Shakyamuni, explored the causes of suffering in life and attributed all suffering to desire (or physical desire). Shakyamuni concluded that to be "transcended," the material world should be regarded as an illusion instead of reality. Therefore, for Buddhists, the material world must be managed in order to get rid of it, and it is not worth exploring.

These descriptions show that most religions in ancient times were polytheistic and regarded many of the creatures on the earth as gods. In these religions, people are looking for a god, but in the end, they could not find the one true God. However, there is another group of religions in the world that does worship the only true God. This group began with Abraham, the ancestor of the Jews. Abraham was chosen by God, and his descendants are those who now practice Judaism, Islam, and Christianity. What each of these religions has in common—besides their common ancestor, Abraham—is the belief that everything in the universe was created by the one true God and that everything He created is beautiful. Among these three religions, Christianity is unique. Christianity believes that Jesus Christ is the Son of God, one member of the "Trinity" (see Appendix 1). To redeem the sins of mankind, Jesus became flesh and was born into the world as a human, as the Son of Man. He was crucified and then was raised from the dead three days later: "Those who believe in Jesus become children of God and have eternal life" (see John 1:12).

It has been documented that religious belief has had an important influence on the development of science. The Greeks believed there was a god or goddess behind everything that happened on the earth, so, in their minds, there was no need to study or observe why things happened. If other religions worshiped the god of thunder, it would then be unnecessary to study why, scientifically speaking, lightning strikes occurred. The worship of "giant trees" would not promote any study of why such trees grow so tall, and so on. As the ancient Egyptians regarded frogs as gods, it would have been impossible for them to dissect a frog and study it. So initially, some science could never have developed or flourished in a polytheistic culture.

When people observed the natural world through the lens of the ancient beliefs we have discussed, the one true God could not be found. Therefore, God has revealed to mankind the Word— the Bible—written by His chosen prophets throughout the ages. Through His Word, He has told the world that He is the one true God.

Another important concept is that although God created all things in the universe, He is separate from His creation. No part of the creation can represent Him. God told Moses that His people should not bow down to any idol, nothing between the heaven and the earth. When we do not view the creatures God made as gods, people can then study the natural world. In addition, Roman Catholic Church also encourages people to study the natural world, so natural sciences developed and flourished in Western Christian countries. Christianity holds that the eternal power and divine nature of God can be seen through the natural world that was created by God.[8] That makes it worth exploring.

The mid-nineteenth century was an important period of enlightenment for natural history. At that time, however, the theory of evolution emerged before a complete understanding of biology was established. This theory mistakenly overestimates an animal's ability to adapt to changes in the environment, believing the animal has the ability to change itself. Therefore, the theory of evolution is not entirely correct. The original intention of scientific research was to understand God's eternal power, but the theory of evolution denies God's power and exaggerates the abilities of living things.

As a result, at the beginning of the twentieth century, atheism rose to prominence, and evolution was its theoretical basis. With the advancement of microbiology in modern times, many scientists have now proposed the theory of intelligent design9 to refute the theory of evolution. The focus of this book is to prove that the theory of evolution is not perfect. In the beginning, the only true God created the heavens and the earth and everything on earth.

When we look at all other religions in the world aside from Christianity, we see that people are looking for "god" in their own minds. Pastor Stephen Tong has said: *"The true God created man; false gods were created by man."* Only Christianity demonstrates that God is looking for people. All people in the world have been created by the one true God, and we are all children of God. Christianity values the relationship between the heavenly Father and His children here on earth. There is only one Source of truth in the world, and that is God, who is absolute, universal, and eternal.

Jesus Christ Is the Truth

The conclusion of philosophers is the ordinary revelation from God, which is learned from the results of observing nature. The apostle Paul declared in Romans 1:20 (NIV):

For since the creation of the world God's invisible qualities— his eternal power and divine nature—have been clearly seen, being understood from what has been made, so that people are without excuse.

So, why don't people know or refuse to know God's eternal power and divine nature? It's because when original sin[10] entered the world, God (spirit) left man, and it became unclear that God created all things in the universe, including man, because of God's love. In order for God to restore people's close relationship with Him, in the Old Testament era, God chose the prophets[11] to tell the Israelites about His creation, the fall of man, and the prophecy of salvation. Among them, the most direct method of salvation is that God Himself came into the world as a man and told the world what kind of God He is. The prophets recorded these things in the Old Testament of the Bible.

The famous British scholar C.S. Lewis (1898–1963) used the relationship between the dramatic characters in Hamlet and the author of the play, William Shakespeare (1564–1616), as a metaphor to explain the relationship between God and mankind. It is impossible for the characters in a play such as Hamlet to know who Shakespeare is. The only way would be for Shakespeare to include himself as a character in the play. In the same way, we can regard God as the Screenwriter of human history. It is impossible for people to truly know God completely unless God Himself sent His own Son, Jesus, "incarnate" into the world. According to Old Testament prophecies, the God the Son, Jesus, was to be born in Bethlehem as a descendant of King David.

In the New Testament, Jesus was born in just this way, and He began His ministry at the age of thirty, preaching the Gospel of the Kingdom of heaven. When people heard His words and saw His miracles—His healing of the sick, His casting out of demons, and His raising of the dead—they knew that He was God. These miracles and His teachings are recorded in the four gospels found at the beginning of the New Testament (Matthew, Mark, Luke, and John).

The secret of creation is beyond the comprehension of the limited mind of man. Hence, it is impossible for scientists to fully understand the truth of the creation of the universe. Therefore, the teaching of "Tao," or the "Logos," or the Truth, can only be learned through the special revelation of God. The Bible directly points to Jesus Christ as the Source of creation. The Bible declares this:

In the beginning was the Word and the Word was with God, and the Word was God. He was with God in the beginning. Through him all things were made; without him nothing was made that has been made. —John 1:1–3 NIV)

This passage in English translation use the Word refer to Jesus Christ. In the Chinese translation uses "Tao" and it as similar meaning as" Logos" in Greek. Jesus created all things, and "without him nothing was made that has been made.

God's words and His deeds are simultaneous: "*For he spoke, and it came to be; he commanded, and it stood firm*" (Psalm 33:9 NIV).

In the last few verses of the thirteenth chapter of John's gospel, Jesus and His disciples were finishing the Last Supper. Jesus told His disciples there was not much time before He would leave them. The disciples could not reach the place where Jesus was going, He said, but later they would follow Him there. Jesus saw that they were sad, so Jesus said:

"Do not let your hearts be troubled. You believe in God; believe also in me. My Father's house has many rooms; if that were not so, would I have told you that I am going there to prepare a place for you? And if I go and prepare a place for you, I will come back and take you to be with me that you also may be where I am." —John 14:1–3 NIV

The apostle Thomas asked Jesus: *"Lord, we don't know where you are going, so how can we know the way?"* (John 14:5 NIV)

Jesus answered, *"I am the way and the truth and the life. No one comes to the Father except through me"* (John 14:6 NIV).

Jesus is the Truth. He is also the Tao, who was with God in the beginning. Tao is the true God, the absolute Truth. God created all things in the universe, and the theory of creation is an eternal truth. This book will discuss the theory of creation based on the Bible and recent scientific discoveries, proving that the "theory" of creation is the truth. On the other hand, the theory of evolution, which humans inferred, has not been based on the results of biological experiments; it is not a truth.

The Direction of This Book

This book is divided into four chapters. The first chapter discusses the formation of the heavens and earth and describes how scientists have proven the universe was created by God. It not only proves the existence of the Big Bang, but it also proves that the words of Genesis 1:1 (NIV—"I*n the beginning God created the heavens and the earth*"—are fact. Scientists admit that the Big Bang is a scientific "singularity," and the existing laws of physics cannot be applied to this point, which means that scientists are unable to explain the source of this point. This book elaborates that everything in the creation of the universe has a purpose, created by God's love for mankind.

The second chapter will illustrate that the evolution theory is fallible and deficient. God's initial creation of plants and animals were all fully mature and each was created according to its own kind (eliminating the need for evolution); this mystery of creation cannot be explained by modern biology. We have defined this mystery of creation as the "biological singularity.".

Regarding the initial creation of mature plants, God's creative power was demonstrated in the account of the Korah rebellion. Overnight, only the staff (cane) of *"the tribe of Levi, had not only sprouted but had budded, blossomed and produced almonds"* (Numbers 17:8 NIV). Furthermore, the initial creation of mature animals was proven to be true by the discovery of massive fossils from the Cambrian explosion.

The third chapter of this book discusses the theory of intelligent design[9] and the theory of evolution, describing scientists' discovery that even the simplest organisms have the characteristics of "intelligent design." The DNA in living organisms[10] is very similar to a computer's digital program, and the programs stored the information of making life. To write a program requires a "program designer." In the same way, the creation of a strand of DNA requires a Creator. Nowadays, scientists all know that the theoretical basis of the theory of evolution is based on the limited technological level of science at that time, when scientists did not know much about cell structure. Since the 1950s, however, the rapid progress of microbiology and the understanding of organisms and their cell structures have made many biologists realize that the wonderfully complicated structure of organisms cannot have just sprung from evolution. The Bible clearly points out that everything in the universe was created by "the word of God."[11,12]

Charles Darwin based his observation of small animals and made the inexplicable leap of taking micro-evolution to macro-evolution without sound scientific evidence to do so.

In the fourth chapter, we will discuss the ultimate creation of God: the human body. All the tissues, organs, and systems of the human body were designed completely, complicatedly, and delicately. All of them come from an intelligent design—an "irreducible complexity design"—which cannot be simplified. All designs are purposeful and based on love, providing all necessary functions for people to enjoy life while being protected.

Scripture Meditation

God said to Moses, *"I AM WHO I AM"* (Exodus 3:14a)

"I am the Alpha and the Omega," says the Lord God, *"who is, and who was, and who is to come, the Almighty."* (Revelation 1:8)

"For God so loved the world that he gave his one and only Son, that whoever believes in him shall not perish but have eternal life. 17 For God did not send his Son into the world to condemn the world, but so to save the world through him." (John 3:16-17)

"To the Jews who had believed him, Jesus said, "If you hold to my teachings, you are really my disciples. Then you will know the truth, and the truth will set you free." (John 8:31-32).

Chapter 1

The Formation of the Heavens and the Earth

When, as a child, you heard the nursery rhyme "Twinkle, Twinkle, Little Star," were you fanciful, curious about that little star in the sky?

Twinkle, twinkle, little star,
How I wonder what you are!
Up above the world so high,
Like a diamond in the sky.
Twinkle, twinkle, little star,
How I wonder what you are!

At different ages, we have different feelings about the starry sky. If there were no stars and no moon in the night sky, how bleak and boring it would be. Romantic evenings under the night sky would be lost to lovers. There would be no joyous festivals under the moon.[13] And poets would lose their starry muse.

As you grew older, did you wonder how our dynamic universe came into being? How were the heavens and earth formed? Though many ancient myths and modern scientists have attempted to answer these questions, only the Bible has given the definitive answers.

The book of Genesis, written by Moses 3,500 years ago, declared, "*In the beginning God created the heavens and the earth*" (Genesis 1:1 NIV). This belief was generally accepted in the Western world as truth for many centuries.

However, due to the limitations of human ability and the slow progress of science and technology, biblical claims were not able to be "verified" until the twentieth century, when scientists confirmed that the universe was created by the Big Bang, thus giving definitive proof that biblical claims were correct.

We will discuss the process of scientists' exploration of the universe, from the initial belief that earth was flat, to the geocentric model, and finally to the heliocentric theory. We will include Isaac Newton's discovery of gravity, discoveries beyond the Milky Way, Einstein's theory of relativity, the profs of the Big Bang theory, and our current understanding of the universe today.

Finally, this chapter uses scientific discoveries to prove that God created the universe and everything in it: The Bible's claim that "*In the beginning God created the heavens and the earth*" (Genesis 1:1 NIV) is a fact. All creation has been precisely designed by God. The Big Bang is the starting point of God's creation of "universe, time, and space," and a singularity that scientists cannot explain is the creation: "*By faith we understand that the universe was formed at God's command, so that what is seen was not made out of what was visible*" (Hebrews 11:3 NIV).

"Blind Men Feeling an Elephant"

To use a common metaphor, from ancient times to the present, people have observed the universe like "blind men feeling an elephant." This is because the distance the naked eye can see is limited. Human understanding of the universe throughout recorded human history can be divided into the following stages:

1. The earth is flat: one's own location is the center of the universe. Ancient human beings were limited to a certain place on the earth due to primitive means of transportation, as well as because the earth is very large (12,756 kilometers in diameter). They believed the earth was a fixed platform, with the place where they lived being the center of the universe. From the Egyptians, to the Babylonians, to the Chinese and Asian cultures, they all believed the place where they lived was the center of the universe. The Chinese even took to naming their country "China," meaning "center country.

2. The earth is round and the center of the universe (geocentric model). The discovery that the earth is round can be attributed to astronomers in Greece. In fact, the Greeks, who were accustomed to sailing, had long suspected the surface of the earth is curved, because they often saw ships appearing on a horizontal line in the distance, first seeing the sails and then the hull of the boats.

The philosopher Aristotle (384–322 BC) believed that planets travel around the earth in a circular orbit. He believed lunar eclipses occurred when the earth was between the moon and the sun. When he observed a lunar eclipse, he saw the circular shadow of the earth on the moon was an arc, and he guessed that the earth might be round

As early as 1,500 BC, long before Aristotle, in the Bible it was written:

"*He spreads out the northern skies over empty space; he suspends the earth over nothing*" (Job 26:7 NIV)

In the book of Isaiah, written about 700 BC, also before Aristotle, the prophet stated that the earth is round: "*He sits enthroned above the circle of the earth, and its people are like grasshoppers. He stretches out the heavens like a canopy, and spreads them out like a tent to live in*" (Isaiah 40:22 NIV)

The view that the earth is a sphere suspended in the air was unimaginable by both ancient Chinese cultures and early Western culture and was not universally accepted at the time of the Old Testament writing. At that time, people thought that everywhere people lived facing the sky. *They thought: If the earth is round, how could people live on the opposite side of me and not fall out into empty space?*

The actual proof that the earth is a round body was not confirmed until the sixteenth century, when the Portuguese sailing explorer Ferdinand Magellan (1480–1521) sailed around the earth. The sailors on his ship went to sea from Europe. The ship did not turn in its direction, and the sea through which it passed was flat, and yet the ship and its crew safely returned to Europe three and a half years later. They were surprised to have returned to their place of departure.

People can see the "sky" with the naked eye. During the day, the sun rises, and then the moon and stars appear at sunset. The positions of the stars and constellations in the sky seem to return to their original places after a period of time. Therefore, it was believed that the sun, moon, and stars revolve around the earth.

By the second century AD, the Greek astronomer Ptolemy (87–105) constructed a model of planetary movement: the sun, the moon, and five other planets in large circular orbits, plus smaller circular orbits (epicycles) orbiting the earth. This was a very complicated model, and it was proven wrong in later days.

3. The sun is the center of the universe (heliocentric theory):

The geocentric model was disproven by the Polish priest Copernicus (1473–1543) at the beginning of the sixteenth century. His book was published in 1543, the year after his death. The book not only explained that the earth and the five planets revolved around the sun—the heliocentric theory—but it also pointed out that the closer the planet is to the sun, the faster it moves in its orbit. This sun-centered view (the heliocentric theory) was revolutionary. However, Copernicus still believed the orbits of the planets were circular.

At the beginning of the seventeenth century, German astronomer Johannes Kepler (1571–1630) determined that there was a kind of magnetism between the planets (the universal gravitation proposed by Newton much later) that maintained the distance between them. He guessed the orbit of the planets was oval rather than circular. Kepler's analysis of actual observations made by the Danish astronomer Tyche Brahe (1546–1601) confirmed his ideas. Planets orbit the sun in elliptical orbits. This discovery disproved the idea that celestial bodies only followed perfect circular motions, an idea that had been held for thousands of years.

Using a Telescope to Observe the Sky

With the invention and improvement of telescopes, astronomical observations have become more and more clear. Only then were there more advanced and accurate theories. Scientist Galileo Galilee (1564–1642) not only studied the movement of objects on the ground, but he also watched the movement of celestial bodies. In 1609, Galileo was the first scientist to use a telescope to watch the movement of celestial bodies. He said his invention of the telescope came from the inspiration of God. Galileo's observations of countless planets in the Milky Way proved the universe was much larger than ordinary people had imagined at the time. Observing the uneven valleys on the surface of the moon and even discovering sunspots proved to Galileo that the celestial bodies were not as perfect as theologians believed at the time. Galileo's observations proved that Copernican's heliocentric theory was correct, and the public soon began to accept Galileo's arguments. His arguments, however, aroused opposition from the Catholic Church. In 1616, the Church declared that Copernicus's heliocentric theory was wrong.

This announcement by the Roman Catholic Church at that time showed that religious leaders valued their status too much and did not respect the discoveries of scientists. This was one of the reasons some scientists did not believe in God. Another reason some scientists did not believe in God was their inability to fully understand the truth of everything in the universe.

Isaac Newton's Universe—the Gravitational Field

Sir Isaac Newton (1642–1727) discovered the three laws of motion of an object. A force is required to set an object in motion. Newton discovered the gravitation (gravity) force when he observed an apple fall to the ground. The gravitational field determines the orbit and direction of a celestial body's motion.   The successful application of Newtonian mechanics to the movement of celestial bodies makes people believe the universe is like a "big machine," constantly operating according to a certain law of motion. And because it is a "machine," a designer and an operator must be needed—who is God. In addition, people understood that celestial bodies were perpetual, and that they were static, not changing. According to Newton's law of motion, an object must be forced to move, and then it would start moving. Therefore, the question became: Who pushed these stars to start to move in the beginning?

From this point of view, Newton is believed to be the first promoter of God. Newton believed that planets can keep moving in their orbits by the law of universal gravitation, but they cannot find their orbits by themselves in the beginning. So, Newton wrote in his book "*Philosophiæ Naturalis Principia Mathematica*" (*Mathematical Principles of Natural Philosophy*):

Through these bodies may indeed continue in their orbits by the mere laws of gravity, yet they could by no means have first derives regular position of the orbits themselves from those laws. Thus, this most beautiful system, of the sun, comets and the planets could only proceed from the counsel and dominion of an intelligent and powerful being.

This statement tells us that the original arrangement of the solar system was based on the wisdom and power of God.

What Newton and the scientists at that time could not understand was that if celestial bodies moved by gravity, why did the outermost planets in the universe not experience outward pull, but only inward gravity, and not shrink inward? The planets inside also have different sizes and unequal pulls, and the pulls cannot be balanced, so they will move relative to each other. The effect of the gravitational field will eventually pull all the planets together, but observations over thousands of years have shown that this is not the case. What is the reason? In order to explain this phenomenon, Newton believed that the universe created by God was so vast and boundless from the beginning, and that time and space were infinite. This infinity and eternity are exactly what the church thinks of God today: God has infinite power and wisdom. How God created the universe is beyond the imagination of humans with limited wisdom. Although Newton and the scientists at that time noticed the effects of gravity and measured the acceleration of gravity, but what is gravity? It was still a mystery at the time.

Newton believed the universe, created by God, was large from the very beginning. The universe has no boundaries, and time and space are infinite. Infinity and eternity do represent the view of the Roman Catholic Church at that time: *"God has infinite power and wisdom."*

Albert Einstein's Universe

Albert Einstein (1879–1955) published General Relativity in 1915. The general theory of relativity holds that the attraction between two objects is such that they each affect the space and time in which they exist—and gravity is the result of this effect.

Imagine drawing a grid of squares on a canvas to represent time and space. If the canvas is stretched out flat and there are no objects on it, all squares are the same. If a heavy object, representing the sun or a star, is placed on top of the canvas, the canvas beneath it will bend, distorting the original grid and forming a "pit." The heavier the object, the larger the "pit."

Einstein pointed out that when a heavier object bends spacetime, it affects the trajectory of lighter objects. If a ping-pong ball, representing Earth or another planet, rolls toward the heavier object, representing the Sun, if it's moving too slowly, it will fall into the pit (the Sun's surface). If it's moving too fast, it will slightly enter the bend, then change direction and continue on its way. When the ping-pong ball's speed is just right, it will orbit the Sun in the correct bend (orbit). And when there's no friction as the ping-pong ball rolls across the canvas, the "planet" will orbit the Sun indefinitely.

The equations describing gravity that Einstein derived were simpler than Newton's equations and more accurate when applied to the motion of celestial bodies. For example, the calculated orbit of Mercury was exactly the same as the observed one.

Einstein's equations of general relativity show that the universe is expanding. Otherwise, all the planets would eventually be attracted to each other, drawn closer together, and eventually fall into a vast "pit" . This question also puzzled Newton when he discovered the theory of universal gravitation. However, Einstein, deeply influenced by Newton, added a cosmological constant to the equations to counteract the force of expansion.

Discovering a Galaxy beyond the Milky Way

After Newton's time, scientific telescopes continued to improve. Many astronomers devoted themselves to observing increasingly distant galaxies and attempting to formulate theories about star and galaxy formation. From the 18th to the 19th century, astronomers were unable to observe nebulae beyond the range of elliptical nebulae observed by German philosopher Immanuel Kant (1724-1804).

In the early 1910s, female astronomer Henrietta Leavitt (1868–1921) discovered a kind of star known as Cepheid Variable stars in the night sky. The brightness of these variable stars emits periodic changes (changes in frequency). The brightness of a variable star is proportional to the period of its brightness change.

Astronomers can measure the brightness of this type of variable star by using the characteristics of its periodic brightness change. They can gain a more accurate measurement of its distance to the earth from the relationship between the brightness and the distance (Inverse Square). This new method of measuring stellar distances is more accurate than the previous parallax method for measuring distant stars.[4] the 1920s, the great astronomer Edwin Hubble (1889-1953) worked at Mount Wilson Observatory in California, diligently observing the sky with the world's largest telescope at the time (2.5 meters in diameter). In 1924, Hubble observed a very special Cepheid variable star in the constellation Andromeda and calculated its distance from Earth to be 800,000 light-years (ly)[15], more than ten times the distance from Earth to the average star in the Milky Way. This marked the beginning of humanity's realization that there are galaxies beyond the Milky Way.

The most important findings of Hubble and his team include the following:

a). All galaxies fly outward, away from the earth (that is Hubble flow);

b). The farther the galaxy is from the earth, the faster the galaxy flies away from the earth, which means the earliest formed galaxies flew away from the earth faster.

In 1929, these discoveries led Hubble to put forward the idea that the universe is expanding.

How Big Is the Universe?

Google tells us: *"The observable universe, the part we can see, is about 93 billion light-years in diameter. However, the true size of the entire universe is unknown and potentially infinite. The observable universe is a sphere with a radius of about 46.5 billion light-In fact, there are so many stars that even astronomers cannot count them."*

That's right! We don't know how many there are, because astronomers discover new galaxies every day. Every galaxy and star is moving at high speeds and with regularity. For example, the entire Milky Way is moving at a speed of 1 billion kilometers per hour. It is moving toward an invisible and undetectable supercluster of stars in the universe. The matter that makes up this supercluster is called "dark matter."

Based on the total mass-energy content of the universe, "dark matter" in the universe is 85 percent of total matter. It is this "dark matter" that prevents galaxy clusters from being scattered. "Dark energy" is estimated to be 68 percent of the total energy in the universe. "Dark matter" plus "dark energy" accounts for 95 percent of the total mass-energy content of the universe.[16]

Where does this unimaginable energy come from? Scientists cannot explain it.

The answer from the Bible is this: Jesus' power is used to support all things, as described in the following passage of Scripture:

The Son is the radiance of God's glory and the exact representation of his being, sustaining all things by his powerful word. (Hebrews 1:3a NIV)

According to the laws of motion, this huge dynamic universe required a huge force, a push, to start the movement, and the thirteenth-century theologian Thomas Aquinas (1225–1274) believed this came from God's impetus: "*Everything that moves must have a mover, so celestial bodies move, at first There must be a mover, and this mover is God, but he does not move.*"

Why God created such unimaginable huge universe? The reasonable answer is: God want the universe last forever so that human He loved can be with Him forever, as stated in the Bible:

" I know that everything God does will endure forever; nothing can be added to it and nothing taken from it. God does it so that people will fear him." (Ecclesiastes 3:14 NIV)

The Process Scientists Use to Confirm That the Universe Was Created

As stated above, in the general relativity theory, the universe is expanding; otherwise, all planets would fall into a huge pit. But because Einstein was convinced that Newton's theory was correct, he added a cosmological constant to the formula to offset the expansion force, making the universe in the general relativity theory appear steady state rather than in a state of dynamic expansion.

In 1917, Russian scientist Alexander Friedman (1888– 1925) proposed a universe model based on the general relativity. theory. He postulated that the universe is always expanding and that all galaxies are moving away from each other. This model of the universe was confirmed by American astronomer Hubble and his team's observations between 1924 and 1929.

The theoretical cosmology, Father George Lemaitre (1894– 1966), studied the theory of general relativity in depth in the 1920s and proposed the concept that the universe had expanded from a "primeval atom" originally created by God.

Hubble's work showed that the farther away the galaxy is from the earth, the faster it is flying away from the earth, indicates that the universe had a moment of creation. At that time, scientists debated this theory. One group of atheistic scientists who opposed this theory included the most famous challenger Fred Hoyle (1915–2001). Although he coined the term Big Bang, (the start of the universe at a moment of great explosion); Hoyle along with two other scientists proposed their own Steady State modes[17] to oppose the idea of the Big Bang.

Hoyle put forward a challenge in a radio program at the end of 1940, in which he declared: "*If the universe originated in a big bang, then the explosion must leave a relic of the explosion. Please find out the relic of big bang explosion for me.*"

Since that day, scientists have diligently worked to find the "relic" of the Big Bang. What is this relic? The relic is the residual temperature left by the Big Bang explosion.

One example may explain better why the Big bang left a relic of residual heat or temperature. Consider this: When people surround a bonfire, the fire transfers light and heat to their surroundings in the form of radiation. The temperature the people feel is dependent on how far away they are from the fire. When the bonfire is extinguished, the residual temperature will dissipate with time. The larger the fire, the more slowly the residual temperature disappears. Because the initial temperature of the Big Bang explosion was extremely high, scientists still can measure the residual temperature left by it.

Imagine the universe as a balloon. At first, it was very small. Then the Big Bang filled the balloon with very high "energy" (i.e., temperature), and the balloon expands. When it first expands, the speed is very fast, decreasing the "energy"/temperature inside rapidly. As it grows larger, the more "energy" in the balloon is transformed into mass and the temperature decreases faster ($E=mc^2$). Finally, the balloon conforms to the present universe, with increased mass and cooled temperatures.

Scientists Measure the Residual Heat of the Big Bang

Before the "primeval atom" existed, or before the universe began (before the Big Bang), there was no energy, no matter, and no time or space. Scientists have assigned an "absolute temperature" of zero degrees Kelvin (0°K or -273.4°C) to that state. At this temperature, all motion stops. Scientists currently have no way to cool an object to absolute zero.

However, when the Big Bang occurred, about 13.8 billion years ago, the temperature at the beginning of the explosion was very high. The residual heat left by the Big Bang can still be measured in our day.

When the temperature of an object is higher than the surrounding temperature, the object will dissipate heat in the form of electromagnetic waves, so scientists can determine its temperature from the measured electromagnetic waves' wavelength or frequency. The higher the temperature of the emitted electromagnetic waves, the higher the frequency and the shorter the wavelength of the waves

When the universe expanded rapidly, the temperature dropped rapidly, and at the same time energy was transformed into mass, which gradually became our current universe. In the last sixty one years, the measurement results of "the Cosmic Microwave Background Radiation" (CMB, CMBR) temperatures were shown as follow:

1. Now (13.8 billion years after the Big Bang) the temperature is $3°K$ (Figure 1: point A) or $2.75°K$ (Figure 1: point B):

    In the spring of 1964, two researchers at Bell Laboratory in the United States, Arno Penzias (1933-) and Robert W. Wilson (1926-2013), accidentally received the residual heat left by the Big Bang. There was a constant stream of radiation coming from all directions in space with a temperature of about $3 °K$ (Fig 1, Point A). After 15 years of searching, the US Cosmic Background Explorer (COBE) satellite program announced in 1990 that the temperature of the cosmic background radiation was $2.75°K$ . . (Fig 1, Point B).

2. The temperature was $5.10°K$ (Figure 1: point C) 7.2 billion years ago (6.6 billion years after the Big Bang), as recently measured by the CSIRO Australia Telescope.

3. 9.2 billion years ago (4.6 billion years after the Big Bang) the temperature was $7.58°K$ (Figure 1: point D). This result was measured by the Keck telescope in 1994.

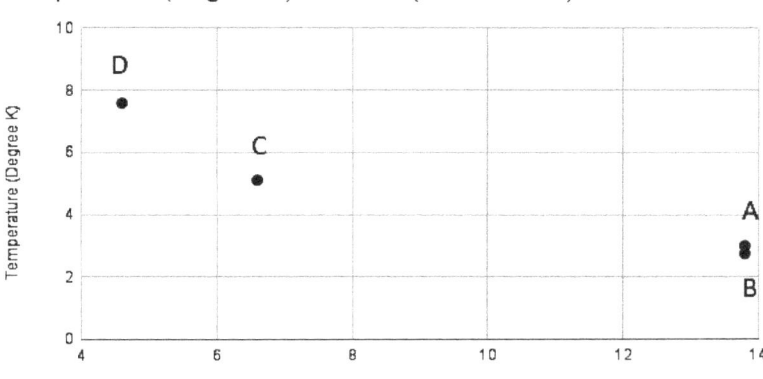

Temperature (Degree K) vs. Time (Billion Years)

Figure 1 The CMBR temperature after the Big Bang vs. Time elapse

The above measurement results clearly show in Figure 1 that the farther away from the "Big Bang", the lower the temperature of the cosmic microwave background radiation temperature. It proved the existence of the "Big Bang". In other words, scientists have proved that "In the beginning, God created the heavens and the earth. "(Genesis 1:1). From the theory of the expansion of the universe in 1917 to the confirmation of the actual measured results in 1994, it took 77 years from the time a few scientists knew it, to the majority of scientists believing that the universe had a starting point–the "Big Bang". But there are still scientists who do not believe it, especially biologists and philosophers. They think that the starting point, God's creation, mentioned in the Bible is unscientific, and therefore they deny all the records of the Bible.

Why do some Christians not believe in the Big Bang Theory?

What confuses me is that some Christians do not believe in the "Big Bang" theory, even though the "Big Bang" theory is a fact that has been verified by many scientists. Proving the existence of the "Big Bang" also proves the God's word stated in Genesis 1:1: "*In the beginning, God created the heavens and the earth.*" This book explains that the "Big Bang" happened, which is why the universe and everything in it exist today.

Usually, huge explosions we see are destructive, so most people cannot imagine that the "Big Bang" can create the universe. Christians believe that God is omnipotent, "*For He spoke, and it came to be; He commanded, and it stood firm*" (Psalm 33:9 NIV). Therefore, they believe that when God created the universe, He said, *"Let there be a universe,"* and the vast universe was *immediately formed.* "This is very similar to Newton's idea. In order to explain his gravitational universe will not collapse into a large mass, Newton had to assume that the universe created by God was so vast and boundless at the beginning, and that time and space were infinite.

Most of the creation described in the Bible is continuous. For example, God commanded the creation of the universe, and the universe has been operating according to many parameters designed by God, and it is still operating now. The universe continues to expand, and galaxies and stars continue to be created.

We will cite a famous example to prove that the author's opinion is credible. Most people have seen the movie "The Ten Commandments". The film's spectacular scenes and outstanding performances are quite attractive, and most of its plot is based on the Bible.

Chapter 14 of the Bible's Book of Exodus records the thrilling process of Moses leading the Israelites across the Red Sea. When the Israelites looked up and saw the Egyptian soldiers pursuing them, they were very afraid and cried out to the Lord. At the same time, they also complained to Moses. Their complaining was both mean and untrue and completely forgot the power of God they have been seen in the past. God once again demonstrated His power at this time:

"Then the angel of God, who had been traveling in front of Israel's army, withdrew and went behind them. The pillar of cloud also moved from in front and stood behind them, coming between the armies of Egypt and Israel. Throughout the night the cloud brought darkness to the one side and light to the other side; so neither went near the other all night long. Then Moses stretched out his hand over the sea, and all that night the LORD *drove the* sea back with a strong east wind and turned it into dry land. The waters were divided, and the Israelites went through the sea on dry ground, with a wall of water on their right *and on their left."* (Exodus 14:19- 22 NIV)°

Here, *"Moses stretched out his staff over the sea,"* and Moses, representing Jehovah God, commanded the sea to part. The sea did not part immediately, *but "the Lord caused the sea to retreat all night with a strong east wind, and the waters were divided, and the sea became dry land."*

From the reading of the scripture, we found the purpose of all the processes of the event was God said to Moses: "*I will harden the hearts of the Egyptians so that they will go in after them. And I will gain glory through Pharaoh and all his army, through his chariots and his horsemen. The Egyptians will know that I am the Lord when I gain glory through Pharaoh, his chariots and his horsemen.*" (Exodus 14:17,18 NIV)

The duration of an event describes in the Bible whether long or short is to glorify God.

In fact, there is no contradiction between science and creation, because science is the study of the principles of the natural world, which was created by God by His words.[18]

Singularity Point of the Creation

Scientists can only prove that the universe was formed by the Big Bang. How the universe came into being is completely beyond human intelligence. In 1970, Stephen Hawking (1942-2018) and Roger Penrose (1931-) published a paper[19] proving that both space and time have a starting point: the moment of the Big Bang, or at the "primordial atom." At that moment, the curvature of spacetime was infinite. It was a "singularity" point with no mathematical solution, a "singularity" point of creation. Therefore, that point is the starting point of "cosmic time."

Our modern scientific laws and formulas are based on the current universe and cannot be applied to the "singularity point" and beyond. So, scientists will never understand how the Big Bang occurred.

Moses pointed this out in the Bible:

"The secret things belong to the Lord our God, but the things revealed belong to us and to our children forever, that we may follow all the words of this law." " (Deuteronomy 29:29 NIV)

Black hole gravitational singularities still exist in the universe, reminding scientists that primordial singularity point does exist.

The most powerful explosions ever invented by humans, including the atomic bomb, have been used only for destruction or war. This is a tragedy for humanity. Only God could create a universe suitable for life using an explosion billions of times more powerful than an atomic bomb.

Today, some scientists are trying to identify a principle that would prove that the Big Bang wasn't created by God. In 2010, Stephen Hawking co-authored "The Grand Design"[20] with another physicist. The book explored numerous theories, ultimately concluding that *"the universe could have arisen on its own, according to the laws of physics, without the need for a creator."*

In other words, Hawking argued that *"the universe could have arisen on its own if all the parameters of the laws of physics were aligned to meet the conditions for creation."* The question is, who put all the right parameters together?

The Uniqueness of the Earth

The Milky Way galaxy is not located in the center of the universe, the sun is not located in the center of the Milky Way galaxy, nor is the earth in the center of the universe. This is a clever arrangement by God, so that the earth is not subject to too strong radiation from other stars and can have a stable orbit. The earth is one of eight planets orbiting the sun. The earth is neither the largest nor the smallest. But the earth is the most unique and special planet among the eight planets. It contains a rotating core that allows a magnetic field to allow life; it is a rocky planet with an atmosphere and water for life. It is in the "Goldilocks" range of temperatures and has a unique rotation. In addition, when we look at the sun and the earth together, we see the earth is very special. The position of the earth is just right for the growth and reproduction of living things. It can be seen from the following three points that the earth has been specially and purposely designed:

1) The Sun is just the right size and mass: If it were larger, it would quickly burn out. If it were smaller, it wouldn't provide enough heat to sustain life. The Earth's distance from the Sun is just right: if it were closer, the surface temperature would be too high. For example, Venus is too hot for humans to survive without water. If the Earth were farther from the Sun, like Mars, the surface would be too cold, freezing any life.

2) The earth's size and gravity are moderate: If the earth were larger, the gravitational field would be stronger, and more toxic gases would remain trapped in the atmosphere by the stronger gravity. For example, ammonia, with a molecular weight of 15, and methane, whose molecular weight is 17, would be held more tightly in the earth's atmosphere, thus building up to toxic levels beyond which life could not exist. However, if the Earth were smaller, the gravitational field would be weaker, allowing basic gases such as water vapor, which has a molecular weight of 18, to drift away into space, as is the case on Mars. Therefore, the gravity must be just strong enough to allow lighter gases to escape while still maintaining the presence of water vapor.

3) In addition to the above two points, astronomer Hugh Ross listed in the book *The Fingerprint of God*[21] that twenty parameters must be moderate for life to exist on the earth. Ross pointed out that the probability of having a planet like the earth exist is one in one trillion if calculated purely by probability. The universe is estimated to contain over two hundred billion galaxies. Scientist also estimates there are over one hundred trillion-billion stars in the universe. In

terms of probability, it is unlikely that an earth suitable for the growth of life would naturally form. All these facts indicate the solar system was created by design.

The Earth's surface is rugged and rugged, with mountains, valleys, plains, and oceans. Land accounts for approximately 29% of the Earth's total surface area. These conditions foster a rich diversity of species and abundant resources. The interactions between plants and animals form a seamless food chain. The shape of the Earth's surface—topography—has shaped our beautiful mountains, rivers, and streams, meticulously designed by God.

Scientists Cannot Create Anything

Scientists may question God's creation, but they cannot create even a tiny speck of dust. For example, let's look at the mass-energy conversion formula derived by Einstein in 1905:

$$E = mc^2 \ (1)$$

Energy (E) equals mass (m) multiplied by the speed of light (c) squared. The speed of light in a vacuum is a constant, equal to 186,284 miles per second or 300,000 kilometers per second (more precisely, 299,792,458 meters per second), so a small amount of mass equals a huge amount of energy.

While scientists can create enormous amounts of energy from a small amount of mass, they cannot convert energy into mass. Einstein's equation is irreversible. It is impossible for scientists to concentrate enough energy at a single point to balance this equation. Therefore, scientists cannot create even a tiny speck of dust. Human power is very limited, while God possesses infinite power.

This brings us back to the question: How did the singularity come about? No one knows. Humanity cannot know anything about anything that existed before its own existence. Similarly, unless the Creator tells us, we cannot know how the universe was created before our own existence. *"In the beginning, God created the heavens and the earth"* (Genesis 1:1 NIV) is a fact.

All creation is precisely designed by God. The Big Bang, a singularity that scientists cannot explain, is the starting point for God's creation of "the universe, time and space": *"By faith we understand that the universe was created by God's word, so that what is seen was not made from things that are visible"* (Hebrews 11:3, NIV).

Scripture Meditation

"For all the gods of the nations are idols, but the Lord made the heavens." (Psalm 96:5 NIV)

You are worthy, our Lord and God, to receive glory and honor and power, for you created all things, and by your will they were created and have their being (Revelation 4:11 NIV)

*For as high as the heavens are above the earth, so great is his love for those who fear him; as far as the east is from the west, so far has he removed our transgressions from us. As a father has compassion on his children, so the Lord has compassion on those who fear him. (*Psalm 103:11–13 NIV)

It is I who made the earth and created mankind on it. My own hands stretched out the heavens; I marshaled their starry hosts. (Isaiah 45:12 NIV)

For I know the plans I have for you," declares the Lord, "plans to prosper you and not to harm you, plans to give you hope and a future. (Jeremiah 29:11 NIV)

For my thoughts are not your thoughts, neither are your ways my ways," declares the Lord. "As the heavens are higher than the earth, so are my ways higher than your ways and my thoughts than your thoughts. (Isaiah 55:8–9 NIV)

Chapter 2

The Initial Creation of Mature Life

In the previous chapter, we discussed how scientific discoveries confirm the biblical account: "*In the beginning, God created the heavens and the earth*" (Genesis 1:1). In this chapter, we will explore the initial creation of mature life.

Everyone, growing up, has asked at least one question: "Where did life come from?" or "Where did all the plants and animals come from?" or "Where did humans come from?" You may have a few answers, but the most common answer is probably that life arose naturally, evolving from single-celled organisms to lower animals, then to monkeys, and finally to humans. This answer, found in human-written textbooks, is called the theory of evolution. In stark contrast, the divinely inspired answer, recorded in Genesis chapters 1 and 2, is that all things, all life, including humans, were created by God with purpose. The first plants and animals created were mature beings. All creation has a purpose; this is called divine creation. In the next three chapters, we will determine which theory is correct.

In this chapter, we will explore the origins of mature life, introducing and discussing the implications of both creationism and evolution. Both perspectives require faith. Evolutionists believe that the vast universe formed by chance, that non-replicating chemicals can themselves become self-replicating organisms, and that lower animals evolved into higher forms through adaptation to changing environments. However, if this were true, wouldn't lower animals be more intelligent than higher ones?

Belief in God's creation firmly holds the Creator's omnipotence. Everything in the universe, including humanity, was created with purpose, not without purpose; it did not come into being by chance, but was carefully designed by the Creator. We will examine these two "beliefs" from a scientific perspective to determine which theory is more reasonable and trustworthy. Christianity is a faith full of hope and a solid foundation, as stated in Hebrews

11:3 in the Bible: *"By faith we understand that the universe was formed at God's command, so that what is seen was not made out of what was visible"* (NIV)

First, let's explore the order of God's creation. After God created the heavens and the earth, His eyes immediately turned to the earth, and He showed great care for it. Beginning in Genesis 1:2, the Bible describes earthly affairs—the earthly affairs that humanity must survive and manage. God's primary concern is humanity's well-being and the environment in which he lives.

God's Initial Creation of Mature Plants and Animals

Scientists tell us that the Earth formed approximately 4.54 ± 0.05 billion years ago.[22] Over vast eons, the Earth's surface conditions eventually became suitable for plant growth and animal life. God then created plants first, and then animals. These creations were meticulously planned and designed.

In the previous chapter, we discussed how the Big Bang's "primordial atom" was the universe's "singularity," and how black holes are currently observable "gravitational singularities." In this chapter, we will explain the "singularity" when God first created plants and animals. Each plant and animal were initially a mature organism. Current biology cannot explain this.

From Genesis chapter 1 and 2, we learn that God created plants and animals in their mature stages as shown below:

1. God created vegetation on the land: *plants bearing seed according to their kinds and trees bearing fruit with seed in it according to their kinds.* (Genesis 1:12 NIV).

2. *God created the great creatures of the sea and teems of fishes in the water, and every winged bird in the sky, all the creatures were according to its kind* (Genesis 1:21 NIV).

3. *God made the wild animals according to their kinds, the livestock according to their kinds, and all the creatures that move along the ground according to their kinds* (Genesis 1:25 NIV)

4. *Now the LORD* God had formed out of the ground all the wild animals and all the birds in the sky. He brought them to the man (Adam) to see what he would name them; and whatever the man called each living creature, that was its name. (Genesis 2:19 NIV)

According to point 1, God created many mature plants and trees on land, each according to their kinds. Therefore, plants did not need to evolve.

According to point 2 and 3, God first created all kinds sea *creatures*, and teams of fishes in the water, *and every winged bird in the sky* at the same time and *"according to its kind."* Then God made *wild animals according to their kinds, the livestock according to their kinds, and all the land creatures* "each *according to its kind."* This tells us that the initial creation of animals was vast and orderly, without any evolutionary process.

According to the fourth point, God brought all the animals he created before Adam. Therefore, they must have been able to walk, run, or fly. This means that all animals were already mature, and the fact that God created animals "according to their kinds" indicates that they did not need to evolve. Therefore, there is no need for macroevolution. All species were clearly defined at the time of creation. Otherwise, they would have become a chaotic mess after just a few generations. This is a "biological oddity" that modern biology cannot explain.

Besides that, after God created the fishes and birds, *"God blessed them and said, "Be fruitful and increase in number and fill the water in the seas, and let the birds increase on the earth."* (Genesis 1:22 NIV)

From this verse, we can see God blessed His creation, and gave the animals the ability to be able to adapt the environment to *"Be fruitful and increase in number and fill the earth.* That showed the micro-evolution ability of animals was from God.

Plants were created for animals. Plants need photosynthesis to grow. Animals also need to move in the sunlight and depend on plants to survive. The leaves and fruits of plants are food for animals. The digested excrement or decayed body of animals becomes fertilizer for plants. The constituent elements of animals and plants are exactly the same, so a good ecological cycle can be maintained. This also points to the wisdom of the Creator.

Plants perform photosynthesis and respiration in sunlight, absorbing carbon dioxide in the atmosphere and exhaling oxygen—just to complement the animal's respiration. Could this be anything but specially designed?

Why are a plant's leaves green and not black? Wouldn't black absorb sunlight more efficiently and make photosynthesis more vigorous? If grass and leaves were black, though, what would the landscape look like? From this point of view, we realize the Creator's love allows humans to enjoy the beauty of His creation.

Proving the Point of "Biological Singularity"

Humans were created after plants and animals. How can scientists prove that the first creations were mature plants and animals? Regarding animals, we will discuss this in the next chapter, in conjunction with the scientific discoveries of the Cambrian fossil explosion. Regarding plants, God's creative power was demonstrated in the Korah Rebellion, which occurred overnight: "Aaron's rod, which represented the tribe of Levi, not only sprouted but also blossomed and produced almonds"(Number 17:8 NIV).

The details of this event are as follows:

Early in the history of Israel, as recorded in Numbers chapters 16 and 17, Korah and 250 other Israelite leaders challenged the leadership of Moses and Aaron. God punished Korah and his men by causing the ground to open and swallow them and all their possessions.

*Let them fall alive into Hades, so that the Israelites will understand that these people are the retribution for despising the Lord. But the next day the whole Israelite community grumbled against Moses and Aaron. "You have killed the LORD's people," they said. (*Numbers 16:41 NIV)

Moses also said . . . *"Who are we? You are not grumbling against us, but against the Lord."* (Exodus 16:8b NIV)

The Israelites complained to Moses, just as they had complained about God's judgment. God's anger was unleashed, and he immediately sent a plague. Despite Moses and Aaron's intercession, 14,700 people died.

To confirm His continued sovereignty, God performed a miracle, recorded in Numbers 17:1-11. This miracle was even more miraculous than the earth opening and closing. It assured the Israelites that they would never again challenge the leadership of Moses and Aaron. The following is a record of these events.

The LORD said to Moses, "Speak to the Israelites and get twelve staffs from them, one from the leader of each of their ancestral tribes. Write the name of each man on his staff. On the staff of Levi write Aaron's name, for there must be one staff for the head of each ancestral tribe. Place them in the tent of meeting in front of the Ark of the Covenant law, where I meet with you. The staff belonging to the man I choose will sprout, and I will rid myself of this constant grumbling against you by the Israelites."

So Moses spoke to the Israelites, and their leaders gave him twelve staffs, one for the leader of each of their ancestral tribes, and Aaron's staff was among them. Moses placed the staffs before the LORD in the tent of the covenant law. The next day Moses entered the tent and saw that Aaron's staff, which represented the tribe of Levi, had not only sprouted but had budded, blossomed and produced almonds. Then Moses brought out all the staffs from the LORD's presence to all the Israelites. They looked at them, and each of the leaders took his own staff.

> *The LORD said to Moses, "Put back Aaron's staff in front of the ark of the covenant law, to be kept as a sign to the rebellious. This will put an end to their grumbling against me, so that they will not die." Moses did just as the LORD commanded him. (*Numbers 17:1–11 NIV)

This also demonstrates that God does not require earthly time, as we understand the maturation of plants. This concept was clearly explained by C.S. Lewis (1898-1963). Lewis used the scenario of a writer writing a novel to illustrate God's absence from time. For example, the writer writes, "Mary left her work and immediately went to answer the doorbell." In the fictional time of the novel, Mary left her work and went to answer the doorbell, which happened in an instant. However, for the writer, the pause between these two actions is irrelevant to the fictional time of the novel. The writer could go for a walk or do other things, then return to his study sometime later to continue writing. God created the universe and all things, just like a writer writes a book, assigning each process the optimal time. God is not bound by the time and space He created; He uses the time He created to accomplish His will. Therefore, the moment "Aaron's rod not only budded but also blossomed and bore almonds" could have occurred at any time that night. Similarly, the length of the days and the intervals between them in Genesis were all arranged by God. It is worth mentioning that from the following verses, we prove that day and night are set by God and cannot be changed.

God spoke these words through the prophet Jeremiah:

> *"This is what the LORD says: 'If you can break my covenant with the day and my covenant with the night, so that day and night no longer come at their appointed time, then my covenant with David my servant—and my covenant with the Levites who are priests ministering before me—can be broken and David will no longer have a descendant to reign on his throne. I will make the descendants of David my servant and the Levites who minister before me as countless as the stars in the sky and as measureless as the sand on the seashore.' (*Jeremiah 33:20–22 NIV)

This proves that day and night is set by God and will never change.

The Specially Designed Atmosphere

The atmosphere is closely related to human life and provides the basic necessities for life, such as sunlight and air.

The concentration of ozone in the stratosphere (7 to 11 kilometers to 50 kilometers away from the earth surface) of the atmosphere is relatively higher than that in other fluid layers, and it can effectively absorb short-wave ultraviolet light. That action protects the surface of the ground from direct ultraviolet sunlight. Ultraviolet light is harmful to the human body, to plants, and to other living organisms. The ozone layer is a wonderful design of God to block ultraviolet light from the earth's atmosphere.

Our air is comprised of 20.95 percent oxygen and 78.09 percent nitrogen. Oxygen is a necessity for animal survival, but it is a spontaneous combustion gas. If the oxygen content in the air is too high, it can easily cause combustibles to catch fire. Nitrogen is an inert gas, having a fireproof function. Therefore, the ratio of oxygen to nitrogen we have here in our air on the earth reflects God's consideration for the human health and safety.

Humans Are God's Special Creation, Made with Love

"God is love" (1 John 4:8, 16 NIV). Because of love, God created everything for humans to manage and enjoy. With this purpose in mind, we can see that God's creation sequence in Genesis 1 is well-planned, not without a purpose as "i*n accordance with their kinds,"* not in disarray. After every part of creation, there was this statement: *"God saw that it was good."*[24] After creating human beings, *"God saw all that he had made, and it was very good"* (Genesis 1:31 NIV). These verses express that God was very pleased with His creation, especially after God created His beloved man.

The creation of heaven and earth and all things was perfect. It was all carefully prepared due to the heavenly Father's love for us and given to us freely. It is not unlike the food, clothing, housing, and other necessities we prepare for our children before they are born (Matthew 7:9–11).

The creation of man was the climax of God's creative endeavors and the masterpiece of His creation. God's creation of man was also a special "singularity point." The man who was created was a fully mature adult who was more attentive and caring than the other animals that were created. Not only did God create mankind in His image,[25] but He also gave man a living soul: "And *the Lord God formed man of the dust of the ground, and breathed into his nostrils the breath of life; and man became a living soul"* (Genesis 2:7 kJv).

"The breath of Jehovah" lasts forever, making Adam a living soul, so man has a spirit, a soul, and a body. Because the human spirit came from God, it is immortal. The greatest difference between humans and animals is that humans have spirits and animals have no spirits. Only those with spirits can communicate with God intimately, and that is why man had the ability to manage all things on the earth. This was God's purpose for creating the man: "Then God said, 'Let us make mankind in our image, in our likeness, so that they may rule over the fish in the sea and the birds in the sky, over the livestock and all the wild animals, and over all the creatures that move along the ground" (Genesis 1:26 NIV). God placed Adam in the Garden of Eden "to work it and take care of it" (Genesis 2:8, 15 NIV). Adam's spirit was connected with the Spirit of God, so Adam was extremely wise: He could name all the animals God brought to him (Genesis 2:19).

God loved Adam and considered that it was not good for him to live alone, so God made a spouse, Eve, for Adam to help him. Adam and Eve were closely attached to each other and became one body (Genesis 2:24). We can see that in the Garden of Eden, humans and God were connected in spirit, and God's love and wisdom enabled Adam and Eve to manage all things. The relationship between God and man—father and son—and man's management of the animals are vertical relationships. The relationship between Adam and Eve is a horizontal relationship between people. With the vertical relationship and the horizontal relationship, the two relationships together form a perfect cross relationship. Only with the love of God can one love others. Only with the Spirit of God can men have the wisdom to manage the earth and resist temptation.

Unfortunately, Adam and Eve sinned against God. God's Spirit left them, and they became mortal. However, because God loves humans so much, He immediately set up a plan of salvation, to enable humans to live with Him again—forever (see Appendix 2).

God Created Humans to Live with Him Forever

God is the living God, and He longs for the people He created to be with Him forever. To illustrate this point, let's try to consider God's love in terms of people's love for cats, dogs, and other pets. Many people treat cats and dogs as their children, and when their pets die, the owners are very sad. In some cases, pet owners have left money or property to their pets when they themselves passed away.

Cats or dogs are adopted by their owners, but the humans love the cats and dogs as if they were their own human children. From what we have discussed in Chapter 1 and earlier in this chapter, we know that all God's creations are the best, and they are here on the earth for us to enjoy for a long time. We know that God loves us beyond our imagination. God treats us as His very own children. God said through the prophet: "*Can a mother forget the baby at her breast and have no compassion on the child she has borne? Though she may forget, I will not forget you!*" (Isaiah 49:15 NIV).

I don't know if you have ever had the sad experience of losing your beloved pet. I certainly have! In 1990, a friend in St. Louis gave us a Chihuahua puppy. I took the puppy on a plane back to my home in Phoenix, Arizona. The puppy looked very cute: His whole body was snow white, except for one uneven back ring on the right eye, so we called him ""*Xiao-Bai*" ("Little White"). He was not only very cute, but he was also very smart. In less than a few months, he had learned to shake hands, sit down, and roll over. At that time, our church often held outings and once a year field service, and so we would bring Xiao-Bai with us, and the children would rush to play with him.

Every day when I get home from work, he greets me with joy, jumps on me, and asks for a hug. When I pick him up, he licks my face passionately, instantly making all the fatigue of the day melt away. We treat Xiaobai like our own child. One day, my wife was playing the piano when Xiaobai suddenly sat down on the floor, facing the piano, and burst into song. It was a beautiful moment. My wife even told her friends how adorable and smart our Xiaobai was.

Sometime afterward, the son of a good friend brought XiaoBai to their house to play. That day, an accident happened, and Xiaobai unfortunately passed away. My friend's family was devastated, and we were heartbroken too. Xiaobai had only lived with us for about two years. I don't have the ability to bring Xiaobai back to life, but if I did, I would definitely bring our beloved pet back to life.

For many, the greatest sorrow is the loss of a loved one. How wonderful it would be if we could live forever with our beloved spouse, children, grandchildren, relatives, friends, and even pets! We don't have the power to do that. Only Jesus can. In John 11:25–26, Jesus said to Martha, "*I am the resurrection and the life. The one who believes in me will live, even though they die; and whoever lives by believing in me will never die.*" (NIV) *Do you believe this?*" What an exciting promise!

The Scientific Adam and Eve

In his new book, The Journey of Mankind: A Genetic Odyssey,[26] American anthropologist Spencer Wells (1969 -) traces our genetic history back to our primitive ancestors, his findings disproving Darwin's "Descent of Man" theory. Wells collected blood samples from men around the world, analyzed the DNA from their Y chromosomes, and compared it with markers caused by minor mutations. The results traced back to the oldest human ancestor, who lived in a small village in Africa approximately 50,000 years ago. Assuming a lifespan of 25 years per generation, Wells calculated that humans had already inhabited Earth approximately 50,000 years ago. This reaffirmed his earlier research, published in National Geographic magazine, titled "The Human Family Tree: A Genetic Test," reference to National Geographic's Project, which uses DNA analysis to trace human migration patterns and ancestry. which argued that all humans share a common ancestor. Wells traced the ancestry of humanity, calling this primitive human the "Adam of Science"; he also traced the ancestry of all women, calling her the "Eve of Science." This scientific method proves that the description of God's creation of humanity in Genesis is correct: "*Adam is the son of God*" (Luke 3:38), and the description of God's creation of humanity in Acts is correct:

"And [God] made from one man every nation of mankind to live on all the face of the earth, having determined allotted periods and the boundaries of their dwelling place," (Acts 17:26 ESV)

Wells was able to trace human ancestry using DNA because the tiny mutations that occur during DNA replication are extremely rare and serve as traceable "markers." The two strands of DNA have complementary designs and carry identical information. This design ensures that during cell division and the rapid rate of DNA replication, the two strands replicate in opposite directions, allowing them to check and proofread each other, avoiding errors and pathology. This miraculous replication process produces no major mutations, only tiny ones that serve as markers; approximately 100 small mutations occur in each genome generation. This extremely rare occurrence is only possible through God's special design, given that the human genome contains 3G (3 billion) bases, and cells undergo countless divisions and replications from embryonic to old age. This is clearly the product of God's intelligent design. Undoubtedly, its complexity is too great to have arisen through evolution.

Scientists Cannot Create Life

In Chapter 1, we explored how scientists cannot create matter, not even a speck of dust. We also know that even if matter already exists, scientists cannot create living things. Everything in the world requires a creator, just as modern industry requires blueprints from designers and manufacturing instructions from engineers to create any product. A blueprint contains the parts and the assembly diagrams for making them. The more complex the product, the more blueprints it requires. Each product is produced piece by piece according to the blueprints and manufacturing instructions. And products produced by humans cannot replicate any other product.

What makes evolution puzzling is the question: *How can matter give rise to life*? In order to illustrate the possibility for nature to give rise to life itself, some scientists proposed the concept of a "primeval soup."[27] This was first proposed in 1924 by Soviet biochemist Alexander Oparin (1894–1980). In 1929, British scientists John B. S. Haldane (1892–1964) and Harold C. Urey (1893–1981) proposed the similarity theory. They believed ultraviolet rays from the sun irradiated the primordial atmosphere, allowing the formation of organic substances such as amino acids and sugars—the materials of proteins. These proteins gathered in the primordial ocean and became a "*hot soup*" from which life was born. In 1952, Stanley L. Miller (1930–2007) and Urey at the University of Chicago conducted an experiment, using spark discharge in a simulated original atmosphere of the earth, successfully creating seven amino acids.[28] Because amino acids are the building blocks of proteins, the idea of a "*primeval soup*" was thought to have been confirmed at that time

It's worth noting that the Miller-Urey experiment has often been questioned because no one has achieved the same results under the experimental conditions reported. To date, scientists have been unable to synthesize proteins because they are unable to synthesize naturally occurring amino acids.[29]

Our recent understanding of DNA has led scientists to realize that creating synthetic life is impossible.

What Scientists Know about DNA

We now know that DNA (deoxyribonucleic acid) is an amazing code of life-making instructions. DNA was discovered in 1869 by Johann Friedrich Miescher (1844–1895). Before its structure was discovered, it was a "mysterious giant molecular." In 1953, American scientist James Watson (1928–) and British biophysicist Francis Crick (1916–2004) published the molecular structure of DNA in the British Journal of Nature. [30] DNA was deciphered, and since then, DNA has been regarded as the "*language of God*."[31] The function of genes and the origin of life can be explained through the structure of DNA. Let's consider the wonders of DNA by comparing the difference between man-made writing and the "letter" in DNA, pointing out how living things can only be created by God:

DNA is composed of double strands of helical giant molecules, and each strand is composed of nucleotides linked by repeated chemical molecules.[32] We might imagine it as a spiral ladder, the two pillars of the ladder each consisting of sugars and phosphoric acid molecules alternately forming a series of three dimensional carriers with information. Each section of the pillar is connected to a base molecule, which is a "molecular character" with information, which can be seen as half of the pedal. There are four bases, which are represented by the first letters A, T, C, and G, of their English scientific names. The four bases can be arranged in any order. Because the volume of A and G is larger than that of T and C, the A at one end must be paired with the T at the other end, and C must be paired with G, to keep the gap between the two struts constant and form a regular spiral. Such two bases form a base pair, forming a pedal. They are a 3D "letter," which has the functions of both "letter" and blueprints. The size of the DNA "letter" is only about 1 nanometer (nm, 0.000000001 meter), which is one-millionth of the size of a man-made "letter or character."

DNA exists in all living things and all cells of our body. We can think of DNA as using three letters to write biological manufacturing instructions. Every three letters form a "word," or codons. DNA is connected by many of these "molecular words." Together, the formation of a long and complex information body[33] is a necessary design for the manufacture of complex organisms. The two strands of DNA ensure that when the cell divides, during the high-speed replication of the DNA, it is replicated in the opposite direction so that it can be checked and checked against each other to avoid errors and disease.[34] All this was obviously designed by God's wisdom; its complexity does not tolerate the slightest error, and it would have been absolutely impossible to have evolved.

Scientists understand that every organism has its own unique DNA. Its DNA sequence can be thought of as a "blueprint" written in a molecular script that belongs to that organism. The DNA of each organism is completely different from that of any other. Therefore, creating a new animal from another requires a complete redesign, not just a modification. Because the basic components of DNA (A, G, T, and C) are the same, some evolutionists attempt to convince people that evolution is correct by arguing that all life descends from common ancestor. However, this claim is absurd and exaggerated.

God's creation is orderly because it is God's will that all plants and animals are "according to their kinds." The theory of evolution revolves around random mutation and natural selection, but the results of evolutionary organisms could never be so complete and orderly.

There are thousands of creatures in this world, and there are thousands of DNA, or "design and manufacture blueprints." Because DNA is unique for each given creature, it would be impossible to create another more complex set of DNAS from existing DNA—just as it is impossible for one book or set of blueprints to modify themselves into another book or another set of more complex blueprints. Evolutionary scientists believe that lower organisms can change their DNA to become higher organisms. Doesn't that go against common sense?

Wonderfully Complex Cells

This section will discuss the complicated structure of cells which will tell us why nature could not self-generate the first living cell. The cell is a living body, the smallest unit of life.[35] Cells form tissues, tissues form organs, several organs together form a system (such as the respiratory or digestive system), and the system then forms an organism. Cells are made by themselves according to the instructions of the DNA in the cell. Cells are composed of many different atoms and molecules. Why do inanimate atoms and molecules become living bodies? This is the wonderful design of the Creator, and there is "the way" in it, as stated in John 1:1–3: "*In the beginning was the Word, and the Word was with God, and the Word was God. He was with God in the beginning. Through him all things were made; without him nothing was made that has been made*" (NIV).

In the mid-twentieth century, the cell structure was revealed by the electron microscope to be wonderful and complex. It is like a micro-chemical factory created by God.[36] Generally, cells are very small, about 10 to 100 microns (μm). Although a cell has a trillion atoms, it is still invisible to the naked eye. The structure inside the cell needs to be magnified more than 10,000 times, or even more than 100,000 times, with an electron microscope to be seen clearly.

There are many kinds of organisms, and multicellular organisms will also have different cells due to the different tissue functions formed. Here we will only discuss the eukaryotic cells of plants and animals. An outer layer of a cell wraps the cell (plasma) membrane, and a selectively permeable membrane that allows certain substances to enter or exit the cell. For example, plant cells permeate and absorb water through cell membranes. Gas and water can diffuse in and out of the cell, which is very important to the life of the cell. Some plant cells have a cell wall added to the outermost layer, which is mainly composed of cellulose. Cellulose is a complex substance that can provide rigid and strong protection to cells.

The cell membrane contains the nucleus and cytoplasm. The nucleus is the control center that controls the entire cell; as well as cell reproduction. Among them is DNA or genetic material, which is filled with chromatin in a double helix structure. DNA can be transcribed into mRNA (messenger RNA).[37] Then mRNA diffuses out of the nucleus into the cytoplasm. Finally, it is transformed into protein through ribosomal organelles.

The cytoplasm is a jelly-like liquid. We can imagine that the center of the cell membrane is the nucleus, and the other parts are filled with cytoplasm. Buried in the cytoplasm are many organelles with special functions. These organelles are designed according to the needs of individual cells. It is not the result of evolution as claimed by atheists. For example, the organelle called mitochondria is the power chamber of the cell. In the process of cellular respiration, it produces ATP molecules, generates energy, and provides energy for all cellular activities. Cells that require more energy have more mitochondria. There are organelles called lysosomes, which are garbage collectors used to absorb damaged or worn cellular parts. The lysosome is full of enzymes that break down cell debris.

Some cells have certain unique structures. For example, the human respiratory tract is full of ciliated cells. These cells have structures of fine cilia protruding from the cell surface, and the fine cilia can move in waves. The fine ciliary structure helps trap airborne particles and expel them when coughing. Such a design shows the love and the wisdom of the Designer.

Generally, plants absorb sunlight to produce photosynthesis. In plants, organelles called chloroplasts are where photosynthesis occurs. Some cells have a cyst-like structure in the cytoplasm of the vacuole organelles, which help to store different substances. Taking plant cells as an example, water is stored in the center of the vacuole organelle.

There are many kinds of creatures on the earth. They were created orderly with "each according to its kind." There are more types of cells that make up organisms. They are different for the different tissues of each organism. It is a wonderful design that can perfectly cooperate with various organisms. The above discussion is only a small part of the amazing design of our Creator. When Robert Hooke (1635–1703) first used a complex optical microscope of his own design in 1665, he discovered plant cells by looking at bark, and then he named them. Through the efforts of countless scientists over the past centuries, and relying on continuous observation and research on improved microscopes, we have our modern understanding of the internal structure and function of cells. This complicated structure and various functions of cells are beyond the imagination of the scientists in Darwin's era. If Darwin knew all this, would he have proposed the evolution theory?

Huge problems would be created if people tried to change the creatures created by God. How could it be possible that the lowest single-celled organisms could evolve upward and eventually become human? How could the smartest scientists on earth believe such unreasonable claims?

This chapter emphasizes that God's original creation of plants and animals was mature, each according to its kind. Each creature was purposeful and orderly, without the need for evolution. The original creation was a biological "singularity." This is evidenced by an event in Israel's history and the Cambrian fossil explosion. God endowed his creation with the ability to adapt and survive environmental changes—the ability of microevolution. Charles Darwin observed the microevolutionary ability of small animals and deduced from it the ability of macroevolution. Scientists have proven that the creation of matter and life is impossible.

Everything God created is perfectly ordered. Everything God created was freely given to mankind for their enjoyment, enabling them to live a good life on earth. God formed man from dust in His own image and breathed His breath into Adam's nostrils, making him a living being with a soul. This enabled Adam to communicate with God and gain His wisdom to manage all things on earth. This, combined with the close relationship between Adam and Eve, formed a perfect cross-relationship.

Scripture Meditation

He who did not spare his own Son, but gave him up for us all—how will he not also, along with him, graciously give us all things? (Romans 8:32)

For this is what the LORD says—he who created the heavens, he is God; he who fashioned and made the earth, he founded it; he did not create it to be empty, but formed it to be inhabited— he says:

"I am the LORD, and there is no other. (Isaiah 45:18)

How great is God—beyond our understanding! The number of his years is past finding out. (Job 36:26)

For from him (Jesus) and through him and for him are all things. To him be the glory forever! Amen. (Romans 11:36)

Chapter 3

The Evolution Theory and The Intelligent Design Theory

The information in the previous chapter about the initial creation of mature life is based on the Book of Genesis. God created all plants and animals mature and each according to its kind. Clearly, macroevolution is unnecessary. Every living thing was created for humans to enjoy life on Earth. God created humans to live with them forever. We also introduced the complexity of cellular structure and presented some arguments that prove scientists cannot create life.

In this chapter, we will show recent scientific findings disagree with the theory of evolution. The "intelligent design" theory points out that the simplest organisms have a structure of "irreducible complexity" that must have come from an intelligent Designer. This theory further proves that the theory of evolution is not based on scientific findings.

The mid-19th century marked the Enlightenment in natural history[38]. At the time, the theory of evolution was a product of an incomplete understanding of biology. In the early 20th century, with the rise of atheism, evolution became the theoretical foundation for atheists. In modern times, with advances in science, particularly microbiology, skepticism of evolution has grown.

The extent of scientists' understanding of the origin of life in the 19th century

In Darwin's time, the field of biology was just in its infancy. Optical microscopes could not see the internal structure of cells clearly, and scientists did not know the degree of their complexity. They thought the structure of the cell was simple and that the formation of life would have been quite easy.

As one of Darwin's main followers, Thomas Henry Huxley (1825–1895), purported: The basic substance that constitutes life is "protoplasm."[39] This is a simple chemical that can be produced by a simple chemical reaction. The ancient and unscientific "spontaneous generation theory"[40] was believed by the people of that era. This is the same belief I held when I was a child and thought that snails were naturally born in paddy fields and earthworms were naturally born in vegetable gardens.

The "spontaneous generation theory "and the idea that the "basic substance that constitutes life is protoplasm, which can be produced by simple chemical reactions" have been gradually proven wrong as science progressed. In 1856, the French chemist Louis Pasteur (1822–1895)[41] researched the cause of wine sourness and proved that it was created by a microorganism contaminating the wine. Pasteur proved that living organisms can only be derived from preexisting life. This theory is called "biogenesis," and it contradicts the "spontaneous generation theory.

In 1953, James Watson (1928–) and Francis Crick (1916–2004) published the double helix structure of DNA,[42] after which scientists understood the complexity of life far better. We also mentioned in the last chapter that scientists cannot produce amino acids or proteins, let alone create life. There was no first spontaneously generated life; therefore, there was no base to start evolution.

The Excessive Claims of Evolution Theory on Biological Evolution's Ability

First, for the theory of evolution to be established, there must have been "preexisting plants or animals"; only then is evolution possible. Another point is that the most primitive organisms are able to evolve. These are the two main points to be discussed in this chapter.

In 1859, Charles Darwin (1809–1882) published Origin of Species: by Means of Natural Selection, [43] which emphasized that all existing species have evolved from previous species. Darwin then published The Descent of Man in 1871.[44] He believed there was no need for special design or creation to explain the origin of human beings: In his mind, humans evolved from animals.

Darwin's main argument was based on the different beak shapes of the finches he caught when he arrived at the Galapagos Islands in South America.[45] Tortoises on different islands had different shell shapes, thicknesses, colors, and lengths of necks and toes. He also found some flora and fauna that were slightly different from what he had seen on the South American continent.

Darwin believed these differences were the result of natural selection, caused by differences in geographical environments.

Darwin observed the small variations these animals made to adapt to their environment, or the theory of micro-evolution.[46] When God created the creatures of the world, He instructed them to multiply and fill the earth; for example, after creating the fish and birds, *"God blessed them and said, 'Be fruitful and increase in number and fill the water in the seas, and let the birds increase on the earth'"* (Genesis 1:22 NIV).

After God created man in His own image and likeness, *"God blessed them and said to them, 'Be fruitful and increase in number; fill the earth and subdue it. Rule over the fish in the sea and the birds in the sky and over every living creature that moves on the ground'"* (Genesis 1:28 NIV). There are four seasons and different climates on the earth, so at the time of their creation, God endowed the organisms He made with the ability to adapt to their environments and make slight changes as needed. This ability is limited; otherwise, it would be chaotic. Therefore, God created them "each according to its kind" (Genesis 1:11, 21, 24, 25). The phrase "each according to its kind" sets a boundary between the species, making macro-evolution[47] between species impossible. We will discuss the details of this in the next few sections and learn that the theory of evolution is a partial and incomprehensive theory. Charles Darwin viewed small changes that took place in small animals, and he extended this out to the macroscopic evolution of ape-man into Homo sapiens, which is definitely an excessive claim for biological evolutionary capabilities.

Problems of Mutation Theory–One of the Pillars of Evolution

Neo-Darwinism combined the "natural selection" theory with random mutation, which is emphasized by modern genetics. The argument is that mutation or a recombination of genes, followed by natural selection, can lead to evolution.

Mutation[48] was first proposed by Hugo de Vries (1848– 1953)[49] in 1901. De Vries observed that in genetic experiments using evening primrose, a new variety often occurred due to a mutation, and the mutation was random. Hugo de Vries discovered that mutations are frequently due to genetic changes, and that a mutation usually is caused by a small change in phenotypic characteristics. This theory is called traditional mutation theory.

Thomas H. Morgan (1866–1945)[50] and his students experimented with Drosophila flies and found that some mutations caused the death of Drosophila, some small mutations had no effect on the Drosophila species, and X-ray radiation would increase the frequency of the mutations. Special mutations could lead to new varieties of the fly, which just involved different eye colors or mutations of wingspan, yet fruit flies remained as fruit flies.

Mutation, as explained by modern biology, refers to changes in the genetic structure (the DNA, that is, the deoxyribonucleic acid present in the nucleus) of a cell. Mutations include point mutations resulting from single base changes, or deletions, duplications, and insertions of multiple bases. Mutations may be due to errors in genetic replication during cell division, or from the influence of chemicals, genotoxicity, radiation, or viruses. Mutations often cause cells to malfunction or die, and they can even cause cancer in higher organisms.

Some minor mutations have no effect or may be beneficial to smaller organisms—for example, bacteria become resistant to antibiotics and insects become resistant to insecticides—but the vast majority of mutations are harmful. For example, a genetic disease in humans, sickle-cell disease, is caused by cell mutation.[51]

Luke W. Huang (MD 1942–)[52] pointed out that the following human birth defects are caused by chromosomal abnormalities:[53]

Humans have 46 (23 pairs) of chromosomes, of which females have 22 pairs of somatic chromosomes and 1 pair of sex chromosomes XX, and males have 22 pairs of somatic chromosomes and 1 pair of sex chromosomes XY. Abnormalities may appear on somatic or sex chromosomes

There is a somatic chromosomal genetic disorder called translocation Down syndrome (Trisomy 21 or Translocation).[54] Two-thirds of patients with this disease may have symptoms of low-energy muscle relaxation and heart defects. Another somatic chromosomal genetic disorder is called Patau syndrome (Trisomy 13; D-Trisomy),[55] which can cause multiple organ abnormalities, brain abnormalities, and premature death in most patients.

As for the sex chromosome abnormalities, if it occurs in a woman, it is called Turner syndrome (22, X + 22, O →44, XO),[56] and it may cause short legs. Even with female signs of swollen ovaries, they produce no eggs, so they are infertile; if it occurs in men, it is called Klinefelter' syndrome (22, X + 22, XY→44, XXY),[57] and it causes men to be tall and thin; they have testes, but no sperm, and are therefore infertile.

Dr. Huang concluded that such abnormalities are degradation or devolution, not evolution.

Darwin's Own Doubts about the Theory of Evolution

Darwin mentioned his own doubt about the evolution theory in the section of the origins of Darwin mentioned his own doubts about the theory of evolution in the section of the origins of extreme perfection and complication in Chapter 6, "Difficulties on Theory"[58] of his book The Origin of Species. Darwin wrote: "*To suppose that the eye, with all its inimitable contrivances for adjusting the focus to different distances, for admitting different amount of light, and for the correction of the spherical and chromatic aberrations, could have been formed by natural election seems, I freely confess absurd in the highest possible degree.*" He immediately gave a possible explanation: "*Yet reason tells me that if it numerous gradation from a perfect and complex eye to one very imperfect and simple, each grade being useful to each possessor, can be shown to exist; if further the eye does vary each so slightly, and the variations be inherited, which is certainly the case; and if any variation or modification in the organ to ever useful to an animal under changing conditions of life, then the difficulty believing that a perfect and complex eye could be formed by natural selection, through insuperable by our imagination, can hardly be consider real.*" Darwin was also concerned about the origin of the first simple eye. He wrote: "*How a nerve comes to be sensitive to light hardly concern us more than how life itself first originated; but I may remark several facts make me suspect that any sensitive nerve may be rendered sensitive to light, and likewise to those coarser vibrations of the air which produce sound.*"

Darwin had long realized that the complexity of the human eye could not be explained through natural selection. And he mistakenly believed that the formation of the first simplest, single-point light sensitive eye was as easy as the formation of the first life (this is another mistake in Darwin's cognition). Therefore, he didn't consider the source of evolution at all.

Darwin's argument is more logically problematic; because organs are not independent entities, they have no autonomy. How could an organ evolve from one species to another?

Creationism holds that organs are given different specific functions due to the different needs of animals. Darwin also knew that "*each grade being useful to each possessor (every eye is suitable for the animal possessing that eye)*"; for example, the eagle needs to fly high in the sky and needs keen eyesight to see its prey on the ground. The chicken lives on the ground and needs only to see the food on the ground, so the chicken's eyes can see a much shorter distance than the eagle's eyes, indicating that the organs have been carefully designed according to the specific needs of each animal. Another obvious example of the impossibility of the individual evolution of an organ is the heart. The size of an animal's heart is designed according to the size of the animal, and it could not have evolved blindly. Evolution between organs is impossible and implausible.

Recently, there was a video on YouTube entitled "Be *Grateful for the Intelligent Design of Your Eyes*" (2017).[59] It pointed out that although in animals we can indeed find the simplest eye, just a light-sensitive spot, compared with the very complicated human eye, two points in the fossil records cannot be explained by the theory of evolution:

1. In the fossils found from the Cambrian explosion,[60] some animals seem to have camera eyes, like human eyes, such as trilobites. The trilobite was one of the major animals that first appeared in the Cambrian explosion. The eyes of the trilobites were very similar to the eyes of modern insects, so the eyes of trilobites did not evolve from the eyes of other insects, nor did the eyes of modern insects evolve from the eyes of trilobites. They were there in the first place.

2. Evolutionists claim that although the eye appears perfectly designed and useful to humans, it is actually poorly designed. The human eye has become a symbol of evolution in two distinct senses. On the one hand, the eye is believed to have evolved with ease. On the other hand, evolutionary biologists believe that the human eye evolved backwards. They claim this is a flaw, because evolution was unguided and therefore had to rely on existing mechanisms, which they claim is evidence of evolution.

Camera eyes are found in humans and in cephalopods (squids and octopuses). The octopus's camera eye has a lens, and it focuses light on the back of the eye to make a clear image. In the cephalopod's eye, its light-sensitive cells, which detect light, face forward toward the lens. In the human eye, its light-sensitive cells face backward, away from the light. Some defenders of Darwin, including Richard Dawkins, have said this is evidence that the human eye is flawed, that it came from an accident that grew out of its evolutionary history and it should never have happened this way. In fact, a detailed study of the eye structure discovered that the orientation of the light-sensing cells is nearly optimum in the human eye. In a human retina, a layer of cells is located at the back of the eye. The eye sensing rods and cones that detect light point backward toward the back of the eye, and behind them are several layers: One is a layer of blood cells, and another is made up of epithelial cells. The blood cells and the epithelial cells nourish the light-sensing cells, which have a very high metabolic requirement. If the eye had been designed the way the Darwinian revolutionists said it should have been made, with the light-sensing cells facing the lens, the blood cells and the epithelial cells would be in front of the light-sensing cells and block the light.

In the eyes of all animals, according to evolutionists, there should be a lot of progressive eyes, with varying degrees of complexity appearing in the history of animals. In the fossil records, before the Cambrian explosion, no traces of the evolution of the eyes of any animals were found. That is to say, in the fossil records, no fossils of transitional animals that evolved from one species to another species can be found. In fossils where no transitional animals can be found, these are called "missing links." There are many "missing links" in fossils and therefore in evolutionary history.

The Atheist's "Blind Watchmaker"

The eighteenth-century English theologian William Paley (1743-1805) famously proposed the watchmaker analogy in his 1802 book *Natural Theology or Evidences of the Existence and Attributes of the Deity*.[61] Existence of God and His Attributes. [61] Dr. Norman L. Geisler summarizes Paley's basic argument for God's existence as follows:[62]

> *Paley offered what has become the classical formulation of the "teleological argument." It is based on the watch analogy: If [someone] found a watch in an empty field, [he] would rightly conclude that it had a maker because of its obvious design. Likewise, when [someone] looks at the even more complex design of the world in which we live, [he] cannot but conclude that there is a great Designer behind it.* [63]

However, the famous atheist Richard Dawkins (1941–) published *The Blind Watchmaker* in 1986.[64] The author explained and demonstrated the theory of evolution through natural selection. Dawkins contrasts the design potential between human design and natural selection, hence the term *blind watchmaker*, for the evolutionary process, which indicates that nature can create organisms like a blind watchmaker would, without the need of a designer.

To object to the idea that the complexity of a creature requires "the intervention of the creator to appear," Dawkins also uses the various degree of complexity of eye in the animal kingdom to argue as if the evidence of evolution were in the book. He started from a simple creature that could only distinguish between light and darkness. A series of slightly modified eyes then gradually became more complex, until he reached the elegant and complex mammalian eye. We reiterate: Dawkins's argument, like Darwin's, betrays the same logical problem: How can organs evolve from organs in one species to organs in another species, because organs are not separate entities? The previous section also used the actual unearthed fossils to prove that it is absurd to use the "eyes of different animals" as the basis for the theory of evolution. Natural selection is the ability of the Creator to give organisms the ability to change slightly to adapt to the environmental changes, but it is impossible to form macroscopic evolution.

The Rise of Intelligent Design Theory

Due to the progress of modern microbiology, scientific counterarguments have been put forward for the origin of life that have not been explained by the unproven "macroevolution theory." The results of these arguments point out that life must come from an "intelligent designer." These arguments are called the theory of intelligent design.

This theory was first proposed in 1996 by Michael J. Behe (1952–) in his book, Darwin's Black Box. [65] Behe pointed out that in Darwin's time, little was known about cell structure and microbiology. Behe postulated that the cell is perhaps the most complex machine in the world, and that it is impossible for it to perform its function without a complete set of parts. The book discusses the properties of the "irreducible complexity" of several biological systems, including cilium, bacterial flagellum, blood clotting, immune system function, and the vesicular transport system. Behe claims that the complexity and biochemical mechanisms of these systems have been greatly underestimated.

The bacterial flagella are the most striking of these examples. The structure of bacterial flagella is as complex as the outboard motor of a ship. The bacterial flagella are only about 40 nanometers in size. Its equipped parts are like the motor, shaft, propeller, clutch, etc. The flagella allow the bacteria to swim. In addition, the shaft speed of the flagella can be as high as 100,000 revolutions per minute, and it can be reversed in real time. Its energy efficiency is close to 100 percent. And it has a signal transduction system, which is a short-term memory system that can immediately move forward in the direction of absorbing nutrients. It is an amazing, high-tech nanotechnology. Bacteria are the lowest known creatures in our world, but who gave them the highest degree of technology—nanotechnology? Scientists cannot create such technology from nothing. In addition, its structure cannot be simplified anymore—if it were to be simplified again, the functions required by the original design would be lost. Therefore, there must be an "intelligent designer" who planned and arranged the cell for it to produce these special functions.

Behe sparked an argument against Darwin's theory of evolution as the only explanation for the existence of life. Readers can refer to "the evidence of biological machine," which includes an animation of bacterial flagellum,[66] to see the wonderful structure of the bacterial flagellum. If the bacterium could understand how it was created, it would say: "*I am fearfully and wonderfully made!*" (Psalm 139:14a NIV).

Actually, the "irreducible complexity" concept was discovered a long time ago by King Solomon (990–931 BC), as he stated in Ecclesiastes 3:14: "*I know that everything God does will endure forever; nothing can be added to it and nothing taken from it. God does it so that people will fear him*" (Niv). The statement, "nothing can be added to it and nothing taken from it," is, in fact, the "irreducible complexity" concept.

Opponents of intelligent design argue that "irreducible complexity" is a plausible argument. They think phenomenon that cannot be explained now does not mean there will be no theory to explain the phenomenon in the future. For example, if a person living before the Industrial Revolution saw a Boeing 747 at that time, he might have thought no one could ever have designed and built something so complex—but it actually took only ninety years of continuous design refinement to create that aircraft. Nature has had 3.5 billion years of opportunity for tinkering, they argue, so the complexities of existing organisms should not be surprising. However, the argument against this is that there were many intelligent engineers involved in the design and manufacture of the 747 aircraft; additionally, building an aircraft is not the same as creating life. The natural world was created by God, and God's creation was completed once and for all; it doesn't need to be modified over and over again, like man's inventions do.

We discussed in the last chapter how only God can create life. After 1996, several microbiological scientists not only discovered that the wonderful structure of microorganisms could not be derived from evolution, but they also questioned the credibility of the theory of evolution from the results of their DNA research, arguing that neither life nor the universe could have arisen blindly and accidentally. Many books and video products on intelligent design have also been published.

Atheist Richard Dawkins also proposed in an interview in 2016 that DNA is much like computer tape containing digital code, genes are digital information, and biology is information technology.[67] Most DNA uses instruction code to make proteins. A living being is a living machine that constantly copies its own code information. Digital information is the product of wisdom—and genes are also the product of wisdom. These views of Dawkins's are the same as those of intelligent design theorists. When Dawkins was asked how the first DNA came about, his answer was, "*I don't know.*"

Intelligent Design Theory Explains the Origin of Life

In his book "Signature in the Cell",[68] renowned intelligent design theorist Stephen C. Meyer (1958-) explored fundamental questions about the origin of life. He asserted that the origin of life was a masterpiece of an intelligent designer.

The concept of DNA as a code was first proposed by Francis Crick (1916–2004) in a letter to his son dated March 19, 1953.[69] In this letter, Crick wrote:

Now we believe that the D.N.A. is a code. That is, the order of the bases (the letters) makes one gene different from another gene (just as one page of print is different from another). You can now see how Nature makes copies of the genes. Because if the two chains unwind into two separate chains, and if each chain then makes another chain come together on it, then because A always goes with T, and G with C, we shall get two copies where we had one before.)

When Crick discovered the structure of DNA, he realized that it is a giant molecule composed of four types of base molecules (commonly using the first letter of its name to represent the base molecule: A, T, C, and G) on a double-stranded helix. Because of the code nature of DNA, the sequence of the code must be correct for correct information to be given. In 1958, Crick further proposed that DNA has an inherent property of "sequence hypothesis."[70] The function of DNA is to convey information. This information includes the instructions for making proteins, and the entire protein manufacturing process is based on the correct sequence of the bases in DNA. Meyer pointed out that this is very similar to the CAD CAM technology used in industry[71] which manufactures parts from digital information

The protein molecules in cells are made up of long chains of amino acids. The arrangement of amino acids that make up proteins has "sequence specificity."[72] This is similar to the "sequence specificity" of both human language and computer programs. The DNA sequencing in cells tells how amino acids are placed in the correct sequence to form the correct protein.

In the growing protein chain, each growing site has twenty possible attachment amino acids (after the protein is hydrolyzed, twenty amino acids are generated). Therefore, for a particular protein, there are many possible arrangements of amino acids. Assuming a protein contains only twenty amino acids, there will be 20^{20} possible sequences for this protein—but there is only one correct sequence.

Meyer pointed out that in the past; scientists used three methods as they searched for the origin of life: chance, necessity, and the combination of the two.[73] Necessity refers to following the natural law. Take chance as an example. By the mid-1960s, scientists had dismissed chance as having any real explanatory power with respect to this critical problem of information in DNA and RNA, the information that makes life possible. Any attempt to calculate the attracting force between molecules to explain the DNA sequence using the laws of nature has also failed.

Meyer coined the term "DNA enigma" to refer to the search for the origin of DNA information; in other words, the enigma is the question: Where did the "functional specified information" in the DNA molecules come from? I believe the answer to this mystery is the answer to the origin of life

To discover the answer to the "DNA enigma," Meyer used Darwin's method of studying the distant past.[74] This method is sometimes called "the inference to the best explanation"; it is also sometimes called the "method of multiple competing hypotheses." To investigate events in the distant past, scientists usually put forward many competing hypotheses, determine all possible reasons from these hypotheses, and choose the reason that best explains the event from the consistent repeated experiences observed over and over again.

According to this method, Meyer quoted some people's remarks about DNA and information; for example, Bill Gates (1955–) said: "*Human DNA is like a computer program, but far, far more advanced than any we have ever created.*"

We know that computer programs always are created by programmers. The information conveyed in any newspaper article or book is always the product of a person's wisdom. When we trace back to the source of any information, it always comes from a person's mind; it is never the product of any material process. Therefore, from these unified repeated experiences, we can deduce that DNA information must come from a wisdom source. Meyer concluded that the origin of life must be intelligent design, the only known cause. Intelligent design is also the best explanation for the existence of the universe.[75]

Intelligent Design Explains Mutations

Scientists have studied the difference in DNA sequencing before and after mutation, and they confirmed it is impossible for mutations to produce species evolution. Recently Michael J. Behe (1952–) pointed out in his new book, Darwin Devolves, [76] that by observing the difference in DNA sequence before and after the mutation, it can be seen that after the mutation, part of the DNA is abandoned, and the remaining DNA is less likely to mutate than the original DNA. Therefore, the number of species of various organisms has its limit. Behe calls this phenomenon "Darwin devolves."

Artificial methods are commonly used to raise or propagate animals and plants, but this can only breed new varieties—not new species. Evolution supporters believe artificial selection provides the best example of natural selection: They believe that after countless artificial selections, new varieties are produced, and in the end, enough of these changes will produce a new species (macroevolution). However, this phenomenon has never been discovered in the entire history of biology. Proponents of creationism, on the other hand, believe this is just microevolution occurring within the species, and that there are limited varieties that can be derived.

Meyer pointed out in his book Signatures in Cells that biologists, from Darwin to those in our current time, realize that living things seem to be designed, but they believe natural selection can somehow create design without a designer. Take the breeding of sheep as an example: The sheep is used to adapt to the environment to produce adaptation. The colder the winter, the more wool will be grown. The breeder can also manually select the male with the most wool and the females with the most wool, and only allow them to reproduce. After a few generations, a sheep breeds with the most wool will eventually be produced. However, the sheep still remains a sheep; it does not change species.

Darwin's view is that nature can accomplish the work done by these intelligent human breeders. If there are always very cold winters, then only the sheep with the most wool would survive to create a new generation of sheep. The result is the same as selective breeding, eventually producing the sheep breed that produces the most wool. In other words, naturally you can act as a designer. We now know that this is the micro-mutation ability God gave to animals to adapt to their environment when He created them. God did not give animals the ability to accumulate small mutations to produce macroevolution, and Darwin and later evolutionists have not been able to explain the fact that there are no examples of macroevolution in animal history.

Intelligent Design Explains the Huge Variety of Animal Species

In June 2013, Stephen Meyer published the book Darwin's Doubt. [77] In the book, Meyer pointed out that a large number of animal fossils suddenly appeared at the same time during the Cambrian Period—that is, the "Cambrian explosion"—and this cannot be explained by the theory of evolution. No fossils of any "missing link" were unearthed before the Cambrian Period. Meyer called this the "mystery of lost fossils" in the book. This is in direct contradiction to the Darwinian evolution process, because Darwin's evolutionary process takes a very long time. During the Cambrian Period (520 to 530 million years ago), within a short period of ten million years, many phyla [78] appeared together, and different animals were in various phyla with different shapes or body structures. According to the theory of evolution, the evolution process requires organisms to make small and slow mutations time and time again before there is a big evolution, and this takes a very long time. Therefore, the theory of evolution has no way to explain the phenomenon that occurred when many animal phyla appeared together in such a short period. Darwin commented on the Cambrian explosion in his book Origin of Species: *"To the question why we do not find rich fossiliferous deposits belonging to these assumed earliest period prior to the Cambium system, I can give no satisfactory answer."* Meyer pointed out that this was Darwin's doubt, and Meyer also used this as the title of his own book.

Darwin believed that the life history of organisms is best described as a branching tree that gradually unfolds, that is, Darwin's "evolutionary tree of life," or simply the "evolutionary tree." Cambrian fossils were unearthed in the Mao Shan Shale in Yunnan Province, southern China, in the 1980s. The leader of the Chinese research team, paleontologist Professor JunYuan Chen (1939–), believes, regarding the "evolutionary tree" presented by this discovery, that each animal phylum has its own "evolution tree," and not all animals share the same "evolution tree."

We mentioned in the second chapter that all beings created by God were made "each according to its kind." Therefore, according to the Bible, each species forms its own "evolutionary tree." Each tree produces branches (different varieties) at different times, as King Solomon described in Ecclesiastes 3:11: *"He [God] has made everything beautiful in its time. He has also set eternity in the human heart; yet no one can fathom what God has done from beginning to end"* (NIV).

In Darwin's evolutionary tree, the base of the trunk consists of a single cell. Common sense suggests that this tree simply doesn't have enough vitality to develop into a diverse array of branches (species). This is impossible in reality, and we can't have a tree as top-heavy as Darwin's evolutionary tree.

The genetic mechanisms of life cannot undergo such a dramatic leap, so any significant biological evolution must be the result of the intervention of an "intelligent Designer." What current science cannot explain is the work of an almighty God.

Meyer proposed the "mystery of how to build animals." Each new animal needs different tissues and organs, and these tissues and organs are made up of different cell types. New cell types require new information found in new DNA. So, the "Cambrian explosion" was not only an explosion of new animal types, but also an explosion of new animal type information. Where did this new information come from? There must be an "intelligent designer," who designed all the information.

Meyer pointed out that mutation is equivalent to randomly changing the order in the DNA sequence that already has the "functional specified information," and the result is likely to degrade the function rather than produce any new function because the chances of making mistakes in changes far exceed the chances of success. For example, if a meaningful sentence is formed by twelve English letters, and the same twelve English letters are arranged in any order, there are hundreds of billions of permutations that will not produce any meaningful English information. Meyer quoted Professor Murry Edon (1920–2020) when he said: "No currently exiting formal language can tolerate random changes in the symbol sequences which express its sentences. Meaning is almost invariably destroyed."[79]

Meyer further pointed out the key question of Douglas Axe's research: "Of all the possible combinations of amino acids, how common (or rare) are functional sequences (that is, of proteins)?" The answer is: "extremely rare." Axe calculated that in the long chain protein of beta-lactamase containing 150 amino acids, the probability of getting the correct sequences of the protein was only one in 10^{77}. [80] Axe pointed out that this small probability is equivalent to a person covering his eyes and using a laser pointer the size of a hydrogen atom to try to hit a point as small as another hydrogen atom in the background of the visible universe.

Another problem that is bigger and more difficult to understand is that to build a new organism, the cell undergoes multiple divisions, starting from the fertilized egg, into two, four, eight cells, and so on. These cells start to differentiate from each other: Some cells become muscle cells, some cells become bone cells, and so on. These different types of cells express different genetic information to construct different specialized proteins. To construct a completely new animal form, all the information needs to be coordinated and arranged, and no mistakes are allowed. Eric Davidson (1937–2015)[81] came up with a schematic diagram of this pathway that looks like an integrated circuit: "Developmental gene regulatory networks" interact with specific genes and signaling molecules. They function to form an integrated circuit that controls and guides the differentiation and organization of cells in the development of animals. Manipulating this process is the job for the "developmental gene regulatory network," to control the time when other genetic information is presented or stopped. So, when the cell goes through these divisions, the correct protein will turn on at the right time. It is impossible for a "developmental gene regulatory network" to change itself to produce a new "developmental gene regulatory network," because like integrated circuits, random changes in parts will cause the entire circuit to stop functioning. The origin and transformation of the "developmental gene regulatory network" requires the participation of an "intelligent designer."

Meyer also mentioned that to construct a new animal form, new DNA information is necessary, but by itself it is insufficient. It requires additional information, namely "epigenetic information," or "ontogenetic information." DNA information is only enough to construct proteins. We need more high-level assembly information to put the various parts together to form a whole new organism.

We know that any information comes from the mind, not the product of material processes. The information of the "developmental gene regulatory network" comes from intelligence. Intelligent design is the only known cause. Intelligent design is also the best explanation. The "intelligent designer" is God.

Science (Education) and Religion

Since Darwin published The Origin of Species in 1859, science and religion have been constantly arguing about where people came from. God gave two "books" to the world: One is His revelation to mankind—the Bible—and the other is His actual creation—the natural world in which we live. Therefore, the apostle Paul said, *"For since the creation of the world God's invisible qualities—his eternal power and divine nature—have been clearly seen, being understood from what has been made, so that people are without excuse"* (Romans 1:20 NIV)

The early Catholic Church encouraged priests to study the natural world, and thus natural science developed in Western Christian countries. Science is the study of the truth of all things in the universe, which was created by God, and theology is the study of the God who created all things, along with the attributes of God. These two areas of study should be completely unified and without conflict or contradiction. God Himself is truth. Jesus said, *"I am the way and the truth and the life. No one comes to the Father except through me"* (John 14:6 NIV).

Albert Einstein, the most intelligent scientist in history, was a Jew who was familiar with the Old Testament. He said: *"Science without religion is lame, and religion without science is blind."*[82]

Atheism, which derived from the theory of evolution, has had many negative effects on modern history. Once atheism became the prevailing worldview, people are no longer considered to hold the image of God, and the doctrine of eugenics, derived from the theory of evolution, gave Hitler an excuse to kill six million Jews. People's pursuit of the enjoyment of material things is far higher than their observance of moral standards. The root cause of the pollution of the earth's environment and our many social problems is also because people no longer believe in God

One of the reasons the theory of evolution has had such a great influence is that the education circle treats the theory of evolution as a "truth" when they educate our children. Earlier, American elementary and secondary school education was dominated by Christianity. However, on March 13, 1925, a decree in Tennessee, in the United States, called "Tennessee's Butler Act," stipulated that it was illegal to teach "human evolution" in any state-funded school. But later, the American Civil Liberties Union (the ACLU) invited a volunteer, John T. Scopes,[83] from the small town of Dayton, Tennessee, to teach "human evolution," deliberately breaking the law to oppose this bill. Scopes was sued and charged to defend his actions in court. Many people swarmed into the courtroom during the July 1925 trial, including journalists from all over the world. They broadcast the trial process to the whole country by radio. In the process, it caused a sensation throughout the United States and the entire world. This was an important historical event in the field of education. It is now called the "Scopes Monkey Trial," or the "Scopes Case."[84] At the end of the trial, Scopes was convicted of breaking the law and fined one hundred dollars

After the Scopes trial, the theory of evolution was gradually introduced into school campuses across America. In 1957, the Soviet Union launched an artificial satellite, which caused the United States to reflect on its science education system. Fearing that the American education system was lagging behind Soviet Russia in the fields of science and technology, the US Congress passed the National Defense Education Act in 1958, which prompted educational publishing houses to cooperate with the American Institute of Biological Sciences. Updated textbooks emphasized the importance of evolution as the unifying principle of biology. By the 1960s, federally funded biological sciences recommended that textbooks be based on the theory of evolution. In 1968, the Federal Supreme Court revoked the law "prohibiting the teaching of creation." Only the theory of evolution could be taught in U.S. schools, and the teaching of the God's creation of the Bible became illegal. In 1987, the Federal Supreme Court also declared that teaching the religious God's creation violated the policy of the "separation of church and state." We can see the results today of this "separation of church and state"; schools do not allow the teaching of the Bible or any religious activities. As a result, some students do not know how to abide by moral law, and they are confused about the purpose of life. This may be led to some of the problems in the public schools.

Dover Intelligent Design Trial

In 2003, the Dover, Pennsylvania, Board of Education passed a policy requiring local public schools to tell students in high school biology classes that "the theory of evolution is not the only 'theory,'" and to give the theory of intelligent design and the theory of evolution equal teaching time. As a result, on December 14, 2004, eleven parents sued the Dover Township Board of Education in Pennsylvania Federal Court for introducing religion into science class.[85]

The main point of this attack and defense in court is the question of whether the theory of intelligent design is, in fact, science. This book will outline the main points of the debate on both sides.

First, the evolutionary scholar Kenneth Raymond Miller (1948–) explained what the theory of evolution is. He believed that the evolutionary history of things can be seen from Darwin's "evolutionary tree." Miller explained the history of life as a tree with species gradually evolving into others over millions of years, producing branches and twigs, a process that gives rise to all variety of life, from bacteria to man. Intelligent design takes a different view that a history of life in which organisms appeared abruptly and unrelated and linked only by their designer.

Evolution scientists thought to refute intelligent design and support evolution was transitional fossils between species (i.e., missing links). In 2004, Neil S Shubin (1950–) unearthed the fossil of Tiktaalik[86] on Ellesmere Island in the Canadian Arctic. Miller believed the fossil was that of a fish (with scales), and a transitional fossil of Amphibia (having four legs) that can grow in water and land, thus providing a factual basis for evolution. However, this example does not deny that the amphibian body is adapted to the needs of the environment. Whether it has fish scales or four legs, it is the result of God's creation, designed according to the needs of animals.

In the court, paleontologist kevin padian (1951-) showed the judge three examples of fossils claimed to have transition feature that support Darwin's *Tree of Life*. One of the examples was "How dinosaurs evolved into birds, as seen in creatures like archaeopteryx which has a long tail and teeth like dinosaur but feathers like a modem bird." The archaeopteryx is actually just a bird, not a missing link. Another example was "How whales evolved from large land animals that returned back to the water". This is against God's creation: "God created the great creatures of the sea" in the fifth day and then God created all kinds of land animal in the sixth day (see Geneses 1:21-25).

The witness of intelligent design theory is Michael Behe, the author of Darwin's Black Box, who explained that intelligent design is a scientific theory. He proposed that some living things can only be explained by design rather than as the result of evolution. The best example, according to Behe, is the bacterial flagella, whose structure is complex but cannot be simplified (irreducible complexity) and has nothing to do with evolution. The flagella have more than thirty protein parts that must be fully equipped for bacteria to be able to swim. This cannot be produced by natural evolution, so it must be the result of intelligent design.

Miller dismissed Behe's "household mousetrap" as an example of irreducibly complex design. Miller took a mousetrap and disassembled it, leaving only the base and clip. The mousetrap became a simple "tie clip," which is also a functional object. But Behe's original point was that removing any part from an irreducibly complex object would eliminate its original function. The simple "tie clip" was no longer a trap; it was useless for catching mice.

Then Miller used bacterial flagella to further refute Behe's "irreducible complexity" design that cannot be simplified. Miller declared that not just one bacterial flagella part can be removed, but more than a dozen parts could be removed and simplified into a useful bacterial type III secretion system (abbreviated TTSS or T3SS).[87] In fact, the two structures are similar, but their functions are completely different: The flagella enables bacteria to swim, and the type III secretion system enables bacteria to attack. However, Behe's "irreducible complexity" design that cannot be simplified anymore means that if a system removes any of its parts, it loses its original function. In Behe's point of view, both the flagella and the type III secretion system are an "irreducible complexity" design that cannot be simplified.

Miller refuted Behe again, and further proposed that the bacterial flagella had evolved from the bacterial type III secretion system without scientific basis, but the bacterial flagella as a whole are much more complicated than the bacterial type III secretion system, and the evolution from simple to complex is an exaggeration of evolution ability. Miller's point of view has attracted the attention of microbiologists. Scientist Scott A. Minich has proven from years of experimental research on bacterial flagella that "in the process of bacterial growth, flagella, whose structure cannot be simplified, appear first, and then the bacterial type III secretion system will only appear when bacteria encounter the host organism."[88] This discovery refuted Miller's claim that bacterial flagella evolved from the bacterial type III secretion system, a claim without scientific basis.

Miller also attacked the idea that "intelligent design theory" is not a science and proposed that the theory of evolution could explain biodiversity. He took great apes (chimpanzees, gorillas, orangutans) as an example. They have twenty-four pairs of chromosomes, while humans have only twenty-three pairs of chromosomes. According to this difference, opponents of evolution believe that humans cannot be evolved from apes. Miller proposed that in 2003, scientists discovered that the second chromosome of humans[89] is joined by two chromosomes, so human DNA actually has twenty-four pairs of chromosomes. Miller believes this proves that humans evolved from apes. However, we know the important thing is the sequencing of the DNA inside the chromosomes, not the number of chromosomes. Evolutionary scholars speculate that the two chromosomes of the apes may join to become the second chromosome of humans, but they cannot explain why they are joined together. In fact, a slight change in DNA sequencing will cause multiple problems. Wouldn't such a big change cause these problems?

In addition, taking chimpanzees as an example, the DNA base sequencing difference between humans and chimpanzees is 1.23 percent, and human genes contain about three billion bases, so there are about thirty-seven million base sequencing differences between humans and chimpanzees. With so many differences, is it truly possible to believe that humans evolved from chimpanzees?

Dr. Luke Huang[52] pointed out the interesting point that humans and apes do not belong to the same species:

"After God created man according to his image, he did not put the title "each according to his kind". This can be proved in medicine that human beings of different nationalities and skin colors belong to the same race and have the same origin. Originally, in hematology blacks, whites, yellows, and reds all have the same type of antigens in their blood cells, so they can be transfused with each other after cross-match cooperation; on the other hand, it is impossible for the blood of apes to be transfused to humans, because the blood cells are not of the same antigens. They are completely different in immunology and do not belong to the same species, so it can be inferred that human and ape are not the same species."

Dr. Huang's point further proves that humans are not evolved from apes: In Genesis 1:26-27, after God created mankind, He never said "according to their kinds".

In this chapter, we have seen that evolutionists, based on the theory of random mutation and natural selection, believe that life arose by chance and without purpose. They believe that the origin of life is very simple, that organisms could have evolved from nothing, from a single cell to a complex organism. Scientists have proven that nature could not have produced the first single-celled life, and that the starting point of evolution does not exist. Nature only exhibits microevolution, never macroevolution, and therefore evolution is merely an overstated "one-sided" theory.

The theory of "intelligent design" suggests that even the simplest organisms possess structures of "irreducible complexity." Intelligent design theorists point out that the theory of evolution rests on the limited understanding of cellular structure in Darwin's time. Since the 1950s, rapid advances in microbiology and a deeper understanding of organisms and their cellular structures have led many biologists to realize that such complex structures in organisms could not have evolved. Intelligent design theory better explains the origin of life, mutations, and the Cambrian explosion than evolution. In short, all life comes from an intelligent Designer.

Scripture Meditation

The fear of the LORD is the beginning of wisdom, and knowledge of the Holy One is understanding. (Proverbs 9:10)

No, we declare God's wisdom, a mystery that has been hidden and that God destined for our glory before time began. None of the rulers of this age understood it, for if they had, they would not have crucified the Lord of glory (1 Corinthians 2:7,8)

See to it that no one takes you captive through hollow and deceptive philosophy, which depends on human tradition and the elemental spiritual forces[a] of this world rather than on Christ. (Colossians 2:8)

Call to me and I will answer you and tell you great and unsearchable things you do not know.' (Jeremiah 33:3)

I know that my redeemer[a] lives, and that in the end he will stand on the earth. (Job 19:25)

Chapter 4

The Human Body Evidences God's Design

In this chapter, we will use the marvelous structure of the human body to further demonstrate that only God could have designed it. In the previous chapter, proponents of the theory of intelligent design observed that even the simplest organisms possess an irreducible complexity, a complexity that must have come from an intelligent Designer. The DNA instructions that make up life are a series of codes, much like computer code. Just as computer code requires an intelligent programmer to write it, the design of DNA also requires a Designer.

I In Chapter 1, we explained that God created the heavens, the earth, and everything in it to show His love for human beings. All of God's creation was freely given to men, enabling people to enjoy a beautiful and happy life on the earth. To achieve this, the structure of every part of the human body, created by God, has a purpose. It not only has the characteristics of "intelligent design," but it also has the appearance to have been "fearfully and wonderfully" made. This chapter presents examples to prove these points. Each tissue, organ, and body system have a purposeful function. All of them combine into a perfect individual body. The purpose of this chapter is to show that the human body must have been created by God, as stated in the Bible.

A Fearful and Wonderful Creation

First, we will use a well-known example to compare the difference between man-made and God-made creations. Many people have seen the terra-cotta warriors and horses of Emperor Qin Shihuang.[90] The pit of the terra-cotta warriors and horses was included in the "World Heritage List" compiled by UNESCO (The United Nations Educational, Scientific and Cultural Organization). It is an amazing human creation. The eight thousand lifesized pottery figurines were carefully processed and fired by potters, using eight common face shapes and making detailed modifications to each face shape, resulting in eight thousand different facial features. In the eyes of the world, those creations are remarkable, but the pottery figurines have no life, and their facial features will never change.

Today's technology can produce various functions of a human robot. However, a humanoid robot has a limited facial expression ability too. The face of a living person created by God can change with mood: joy, anger, or sorrow. Neither pottery figurines nor human robots are anything compared to the 7.7 billion humans currently on the earth, each with different personalities, looks, and fingerprints in the world. What's even more amazing is that genes make family members have similar appearances but still different personalities. God is the Master Potter, creating and shaping each and every person in wonderful ways.

King David (1040–970 BC) deeply felt that he was "fearfully and wonderfully"' created by God, as stated in the book of Psalms:

"For you created my inmost being; you knit me together in my mother's womb. I praise you because I am fearfully and wonderfully made; your works are wonderful; I know that full well". (Psalm 139:13–14 NIV)

The main differences between God's creation of humans and animals are: 1) Humans have a spirit bestowed by God, but animals do not; and 2) Humans have God's image, and animals do not. Monkeys do not have a spirit, where did they get a spirit to evolve into humans? It is impossible that animals could not evolve into human beings.

The human body is a very complex network system of tissues and organs formed by trillions of cells. Each tissue and organ is an "irreducible complexity" design with purpose. Together they form an "irreducible complexity" body with self-function and self-protection. According to medical science, the body is divided into ten main systems: skeletal, muscular, cardiovascular, nervous, endocrine, lymphatic, respiratory, digestive, urinary, and reproductive. Each system has its own main function and other secondary functions cooperatively, "serving faithfully" people throughout their lives, enabling them to engage in all sorts of activities in life, to recognize and adapt to the environment, and to be equipped with the functions of growth, repair, and reproduction.

The complexity of the human body can be seen in the video *"Human Body"* produced by National Geographic[91]. It summarizes the interrelationships and main function of each system as follows:

The adult skeletal system is a framework of 206 bones. They hold the body together; give it shape and protects its organs and tissues. The skeleton also provides the anchor points for the muscular system, which include three types of muscles: skeletal, smooth, and cardiac. They are found throughout the body and facilitate movement. Nested within these muscles is the cardiovascular system, a pipeline that includes the heart, blood vessels, and the blood itself. The cardiovascular system delivers the oxygen, white blood cells, hormones, and nutrients throughout the body.

Lastly the nervous system is a communication network of nerve cells that the body uses to transmit information and coordinate bodily functions. It is comprised of the brain, the hub of sensory and intellectual activity, the spinal cord, and many cranial and spinal nerves that emanate from them. This infrastructure created by neurons, blood, muscles, and bones allow three other systems to regulate the body's environment; the endocrine, lymphatic, and urinary systems.

The endocrine system uses a series of glands that processes information carried by the nervous system to help regulate the body's processes. Thanks to this neural connection, endocrine glands, such as the thyroid, are aware of the amount of hormones and other chemicals that they need to produce. These chemicals are distributed throughout the body by way of the cardiovascular system.

The cardiovascular system and the nervous system are also utilized by the lymphatic system, a collection of lymph nodes and vessels that help the body regulate defenses. Also called the immune system, the lymphatic system uses neural pathway to transmit information about the affected area of the body and then sends out healing agents, like white blood cells via the blood stream

Another key regulatory system is the urinary system, which includes the kidneys, ureters, bladder and urethra. The urinary system, or the renal system, maintains the body's electrolyte levels and filters waste from the blood. This waste is sent through the blood vessels into the kidneys; then it is expelled as urine. All of these systems require energy to function and that is where the respiratory and digestive systems come in.

The respiratory system is a group of passageways and organs that extract life-giving oxygen from the air we breathe. Air enters the body through the nasal cavities and then travels down the throat and is transported to the lung. The lungs extract the oxygen for the body to use and then expel carbon dioxide by-product when we exhale.

Energy can also come from food. The digestive system is an approximately 30-feet series of organs that convert food into fuel. Food enters the system through the mouth, then moves into the esophagus the stomach and the intestines. Nutrients are absorbed into the body while solid waste is expelled through the anal canna, at the end of the digestive tract.

In the following sections, we will describe several representative systems, to understand that only God could design the extremely complex and perfect human body.

God's Great Love: Creating Man in His Own Image

The first book of the Bible is Genesis, which states: ""*So God created mankind in his own image, in the image of God he created them; male and female he created them*" (Genesis 1:27 NIV). The primary purpose of the phrase "God created man in his own image" is to indicate that humans were given dominion over all other living things on earth: "*Rule over the fish in the sea and the birds in the sky and over every living creature that moves on the ground.*" (Genesis 1:31 NIV) Notice that God created humans to rule over the animals; He did not create the animals to evolve into humans. Second, God's creations are always perfect. After God created humans, "*God saw all that he had made, and it was very good*" (Genesis 1:31 NIV).

The human body is perfect in appearance: symmetrical and well-proportioned; possessing limbs and the ability to move and maintain balance; eyes capable of seeing objects in their proper orientation; and ears capable of discerning sounds from all directions and from afar. Its features are beautiful, and the arrangement of its parts conforms to the golden ratio (φ = 1.61803398875).[92] Therefore, the human body is beautiful and meticulously designed. Most precious of all, humans bear the image of God. We possess not only a beautiful body but also a precious soul, capable of communing with God

The golden ratio, created by God, is often borrowed and applied in artistic invention. For example, Leonardo da Vinci (1452–1519) painted the Mona Lisa. [93] Her face and head in this painting are drawn according to the golden ratio, making it a world-renowned masterpiece. It's worth noting that the artist created this work—but who created the artist? It must be a creator greater than the artist himself—God.

The design of human appearance, including the facial features and skin, is not only pleasing visually, but it is also designed to protect the human body and allow people to enjoy life. When people open their eyes, they can see the colorful world outside and its changes. Their vision provides the first impression of people, things, and surroundings. This initial impression gives people the judgment of "like" or "dislike." If Eve saw that the fruit on "the tree of the knowledge of good and evil" was not "*pleasing to the eyes*" (Genesis 3:6 NIV), she would probably not have picked it and ate it.

We can see the beauty of the human body through praise from the opposite sex. This kind of praise can be found in various literary works.

The first seven verses of Song of Songs chapter 4 describe the beauty of the human body; the conclusion is given in verse 7 (NIV):

"You are altogether beautiful, my darling;
there is no flaw in you."

Song of Songs 4:1a (NIV) describes the beauty of the eyes:

"How beautiful you are, my darling!
Oh, how beautiful!
Your eyes behind your veil are doves".

Elsewhere in the Bible, Genesis 29 also describes how the appearance of a girl's eyes determines her attractiveness. Thus, Jacob loved Rachel more than Leah: *"Leah had weak eyes, but Rachel had a lovely figure and was beautiful"* (Genesis 29:17 NIV).

The human eye, created by God, is incredibly complex and wondrous. As we discussed in the previous chapter, Darwin considered the human eye to be an organ of "extraordinary complexity and perfection" in both function and appearance. Darwin attempted to use the theory of evolution to explain that human eyes might have evolved from animal eyes, because animal eyes have varying degrees of complexity. We have already refuted his argument. Modern medicine has proven that it is impossible for animal eyes to evolve into human eyes.

The eye's lens is elastic and can "adjust its thickness" so that light can be focused on the retina at any time. This allows people to clearly see distant or close objects. The lens of the eye and the cornea at the forefront of the eye are both transparent. There are no blood vessels in the lens and cornea, but how do they get nutrition? This requires God's perfect design

Aqueous humor is produced in the ciliary body of the eye, which is transparent and nutrient-containing liquid water. It first flows into the posterior chamber of the eyeball, and then enters the anterior chamber of the eyeball through the pupil.[94] Then, the aqueous humor is absorbed into the scleral sinus. Aqueous humor is constantly produced and absorbed. The amount produced and absorbed is equal. In addition to providing nutrients to the avascular tissue in the eye and taking away metabolites, the aqueous humor also has the function of maintaining the shape of the eyeball. The amazing thing is that the intraocular pressure of a normal person will be maintained between 10 and 20 mmHg. The middle value of the range of normal intraocular pressure is approximately equal to atmospheric pressure

(14.7 mmHg at sea level), which means that the range of intraocular pressure is specially designed. If the intraocular pressure is too low, the eyeball will not be round; if the amount of aqueous humor absorbed is less than the amount produced, the intraocular pressure will be too high. Too high intraocular pressure can damage the optic nerves. In severe cases, it can lead to glaucoma[95] and even blindness. All this shows that the design of the eye has "irreducible complexity."

In the book of Exodus, when Moses was up on Mount Horeb, the angel of the Lord appeared to him. From their conversation, we can see that God is the One who makes people speak, hear, and see:

The Lord said to him [Moses], "Who gave human beings their mouths? Who makes them deaf or mute? Who gives them sight or makes them blind? Is it not I, the Lord?" —Exodus 4:11 NIV)

God designed our two ears and our mouth for us to obey: *"Everyone should be quick to listen, slow to speak and slow to become angry"* (James 1:19 NIV).

There is an olfactory mucosa containing many olfactory receptors at the upper end of the nose. The information detected by the receptors enters the brain through the cranial nerves creating the sense of smell. This is also an expression of God's love for people, so that we can smell the fragrance of flowers and other aromas—as well as dangerous gases. We also have a sense of taste.[96] We can taste the sweet, salty, sour, bitter, and fresh flavors of food and enjoy all kinds of delicacies.

In addition to contributing the appearance of the human body, the skin has other functions. It is the largest organ of the human body, and its primary function is to protect the body; provide resistance to environmental toxins and physical stress as well as thermoregulation through perspiration and sensation; and detect touch, heat, and pain. The skin has two temperature sensors for measuring cold and heat at the same time to control the body temperature within a certain range.[97] Sunlight on the lower layer of the skin's epidermis will produce a chemical reaction to synthesize cholecalciferol, which is vitamin D3, required by the human body.[98]

The skin has been designed with multiple levels of protection to keep the internal organs of the body safe from pathogens or the external environment.

God's Precision Design

A person's beautiful appearance must have a strong supporting skeleton. From the womb to about twenty-five years of age, the human skeleton grows with age; after reaching old age, the skeleton shortens accordingly. How did God design this strong skeleton?

God's design is very clever. The skeletal bones contain abundant blood vessels and nerve tissues for growth. There are two types of bone cells: osteoblasts and osteoclasts.[99] Osteoblasts form bone in a micro-scale, while osteoclasts dissolve bone in a micro-scale. Therefore, a child's growth is the result of the osteoblasts' growth rate being greater than the osteoclasts' dissolve rate.

The bones, like other organs, are composed of active and dynamic tissues with metabolic activities from time to time. This imbalance of osteoblasts and osteoclasts in people result in a renewed skeleton every seven to ten years. This can be observed when a child's body grows taller. When a person goes beyond middle age, on the contrary, the function of osteoblasts will be less than that of osteoclasts, resulting in a 1 to 2 percent reduction in bone mass each year; thus an elderly body may be relatively shortened.

The bones accurately store calcium, phosphates, and other minerals in specific locations to prevent the formation of stones or calcification in other non-desired areas. The bones have the function of hematopoietic in bone marrow, which produces about trillion blood cells every day.[100]

The way bones connect to each other is through different ingenious joint designs, according to the relative movement required between the two bones.[101] There are completely immobile joints, there are micro-movement joints, and there are fully movable joints (diarthroses). In response to the different movements required for different parts of the body, the diarthroses joints have six different designs, allowing each part of the body to perform the movements needed in life

The most amazing thing is that some joints have a magical lubricant: The connected bones are separated by fluid-filled cavities. The cavity contains some viscous synovial fluid, similar to an egg white. For example, the knee joint is surrounded by a ligament capsule with lubricating fluid inside. Without this design, it would be difficult for people to walk, let alone run.

Skeletal muscles are muscles that connect bones.[102] Muscles only do two things: contract and relax. There are 640 skeletal muscles in the human body, and together they produce all the movements needed in life. Actions rely on the nervous system to activate muscles, and each muscle uses its own nerve to stimulate contraction. Muscle movements consume energy, and muscles also use their own arteries and veins to supply nutrients such as blood, oxygen, etc.

The structure of a skeletal muscle is like that of a strong rope. Thousands of tiny parallel myofibrils are squeezed together to form muscle fibers. Many muscle fibers form larger rope-like bundles, which combine to form larger rope-like muscle organs, such as the biceps bronchi. This bundled configuration makes the muscle tissue quite strong. To further protect the muscles, each muscle is wrapped with supportive sheaths formed by several different types of connective tissue materials to prevent bursting. when the muscles contract and swell. These peculiar designs surpass human wisdom and explain why muscles are so strong.

God created living beings with souls

Neural networks are distributed throughout the body to maintain normal operation. These networks are spread over every cell, tissue, and organ. It becomes the human nervous system through the connection of countless 180 billion nerve cells (neurons).[103] The terminus of the nervous system or these networks is the human brain. The brain is like a huge supercomputer, with different microprocessors processing different incoming information, and a lot of memory. The human brain is the command center of the whole body: It receives information from the senses, judges the received information, and produces decisions and make actions. Through the human brain, human beings can understand themselves, other people, things, and the environment around them, as well as the ability to solve various survival problems. These abilities enable humans to surpass other created animals.

The average adult brain weighs about three pounds (a human brain is three times larger than that of a chimpanzee). The intelligence of an animal can be judged by the size of the brain. Based on the size of the brain alone, it is impossible for a chimpanzee to evolve into a human being. Biologists with evolutionary theory believe that vertebrates and mammals have brainstems, and illusively claimed that vertebrates and mammals have a common ancestor; they think that the brains of human beings have evolved from simple to complex. These conclusions are drawn without scientific basis. It is, as a whole, a partial claim. that exists as the excessive claim in the theory of evolution. The size of the brain of a given animal is created and designed by God according to the intelligence required for the survival of the animal (God's creation).

The human brain is the most important and most vulnerable organ of the human body. So, it was designed with multiple layers of protection. The outermost layer is the hair and scalp. Underneath is the skull layer surrounding and protecting the brain. The surface of the brain and spinal cord is also covered with meninges, which are connective tissue membranes. The meninges are composed of the outermost dura mater, the middle arachnoid, and the innermost pia mater. The dura mater is a strong, inelastic film that fits tightly under the skull. There are 125 to 150 milliliters of cerebrospinal fluid circulating in the subarachnoid space between the arachnoid and pia mater, which is replaced three times a day. Cerebrospinal fluid can transport nutrients from the blood to the brain, and at the same time remove metabolic waste and harmful substances. Cerebrospinal fluid can also further protect the brain from damage caused by impact.

It is worth mentioning that God put in place an intelligent design feature called the blood-brain barrier.[104] It is essential for the brain to function properly. The brain has a very high density of neurons and blood vessels. The distance between every neuron and blood vessel is very close, about 20 to 25 micro-meters. At the same time, the brain also requires high energy, consuming about 20 to 25 percent of total body energy demand. Therefore, without the blood-brain barrier, the blood supply to the central nervous system will easily fluctuate or even be damaged by the fluctuations in the blood stream. The function of the blood-brain barrier is to manage the micro-environment of the substances and the structures around that particular area, by regulating the entry of nutrients and exit of waste and regulating the entry and the exit of ions and fluids. To provide these functions, the blood vessels in the brain have special designed structures with three layers of regulations:[105]

1. All blood vessels are wrapped with epithelial cells. The epithelial cells in the brain are created with a special design, called endothelial cells. The gap between the adjacent endothelial cells is a tight junction, limiting the blood stream diffusion into the brain tissues. The endothelial cells also can release peptidases or enzymes that can inactivate proteins or other potentially neurotoxic substances.

2. Basement membranes with embedded parasites are cells wrapped around the blood vessels. They are chemical sensors that can sense the substances coming through the bloodstream and regulate the amount passing through the membrane.

3. The last layer is called glia or astrocytes with polarized feet; they wrap themselves all around the blood-brain barrier and play an important role in the management of ions and fluids. They control the whole of blood-brain barrier activities.

The above-mentioned structures are very complicated, and every layer has its purpose. The detail structures and functions are beyond our imagination. Who could have designed the blood-brain barrier? Only God could have designed it.

There are so many nerve cells in the human body that need to be connected correctly and convey information at a very high speed. How did God design it? We can imagine that every nerve cell stretches out many "hands" from the cell body,[106] to be connected to the "hand" of the adjacent nerve cells. The outstretched "hands" are nerve fibers, and the human body transmits information through these nerve fibers. Nerve fibers form a nerve impulse to transmit nerve information by forming electrical current.[107] The transmission rate of nerve fibers is between 50 and 130 meters per second. (At 20°C, the speed of sound in the air is about 343 meters per second.) Information everywhere in the body can be instantly transmitted and processed because of this. Its structure uses a unique insulation design to achieve insulation and high-speed transmission.

The human body has billions of nerve fibers. For example, the ulnar nerve that leads to two fingers is a relatively small nerve bundle. It may contain about twenty thousand nerve fibers[108] to facilitate the movement of the two fingers. Every fiber in the nerve bundle needs to be insulated. How do you insulate very small nerve fibers?

The insulation between each fiber are nerve fiber cells called "Schwann cells," which are wrapped on top of each nerve fiber. These cells produce fat and white myelin wrapped around each fiber many times. Each "Schwann cell" is about one millimeter long. A nerve fiber may have hundreds or even thousands of "Schwann cells." There is a small gap between each "Schwann cell"; this design not only provides the necessary insulation, but it also greatly speeds up the transmission rate of nerve signals. This fast transmission is called salutatory transmission. This design is beyond human imagination!

God gave humans free will

The Bible records the declaration of the prophet Ezekiel: "*[The Lord Jehovah said that] 'I will give you a new heart and put a new spirit in you; I will remove from you your heart of stone and give you a heart of flesh'*" (Ezekiel 36:26 NIV). Here, the term heart refers to people's "minds." God is omniscient and omnipotent, and only God can change people's hearts.

Where is the "mind" of human beings located? Materialists[109] believe that the human brain is just matter, and it is impossible to produce a "mind". Recently, it has been scientifically proven that the human brain is not only material, but it also contains a "mind." Next, we will quote the neurosurgeon and intelligent design advocate Dr. Michael Egnor,[110] who mentioned several pieces of scientific evidence that refute materialism and prove the human brain is not just material, but that it also has a "mind."[111]

First, Dr. Egnor pointed out there were variety of classical studies of neuroscience to support the fact that some aspects of the mind are not materials. The first set of experiments show that cerebral localization with certain kinds of neurological functions, but not with others, has been known since the nineteenth century. For motor and sensory functions, there are very specific locations in the brain that seem to mediate those functions. For example, moving the right hand is controlled at a specific location in the cerebral of the left hemisphere, and vision is controlled by a small, discrete point in the occipital lobe of the brain. However, higher intellectual functions, such as abstract thought and personality-related traits are not in a specific location in the brain, which means that such activities of the brain are not controlled by brain material.

In his speech, Dr. Egnor put forward the results of the following neuroscience researches that further prove that the brain is not only material but also mind:

1. In the middle of the twentieth century, surgeons have realized that cutting off the fiber bundles connecting the two hemispheres of the brain on patients with severe epilepsy.[112] The operation can prevent seizures spread from one cerebral hemisphere to the other hemisphere of the brain. All the patients, after the operation, showed greatly improvement in their life. There was no obvious difference between the patient's behavior and thinking before and after the operation. This means that human thoughts are not produced purely by material in the brain. Otherwise, the brain, when divided into two halves, would definitely have had a great impact on a person. It is reasonable to think that after the operation, the patient might become "two people." This is not the case.

2. Dr. Wilder Graves Penfield (1891–1976)[113] was the first neurosurgeon to symmetrically operate on human brains when patients were awake, to determine the focus of their seizures and to remove it and stop the epileptic seizures. He operated on upwards of a thousand patients. Penfield observed that no matter what he did to the brain, he couldn't change the patient's intellect, consciousness, reason, or self-awareness. That was a fundamental core of the person's soul, and no matter what he did to the brain, the person's soul remained the same. His conclusion was that the brain is not purely matter, and that human thoughts are not purely produced by the matter in the brain.

3. In 2006, neuroscientist Adrian Owen (1966–)[114] published a study on the function of the vegetative human brain.[115] Owen's experiments found that in patients with persistent vegetative stage (deep coma) the brain can also respond to meaningful sounds. This proves that certain aspects of the human mind will not be destroyed by serious brain damage. That means that the mind does not all come from brain materials.

4. In the 1950s, neuroscientist Benjamin Libet (1916– 2007)[116] engaged in the time relationship between human thought and brain activity. One of Libet's experiments was to find the time interval between the "brain wave spike," when the subject wants to press a button and the moment when he presses the button. Libet wanted to use this experiment to prove whether people have "free will" or not, and he found that the time interval between the two events was fairly consistent for all subjects—about half a second.

When a person is about to do something, his brain waves will produce a spike. When a person makes a conscious decision from an unconscious motive, a "brain wave spike" is first generated, and then the person performs the action. Materialists believed that Libet was misleading people into thinking they had "free will." They think that, in fact, the "material brain" makes the decision to produce a "brain wave spike." It is done by neurotransmitters and neurochemicals.

Libet disagreed with the materialist's point of view. He further asked the subjects to decide to press the button, and then change their minds and decide not to press the button. As a result, Libet found that when the subject decided to press the button, there was a "brain wave spike," but when the person decided not to press the button, there was no "brain wave spike." Libet believed that if the subject decided to press the button, there was a "brain wave spike" that was caused by the "material brain" making a decision, but then, when the subject decided not to press the button, there was no "brain wave spike." If the materialists believed that the 'brain wave spike" was an action made by the "material brain," then when the subject decided not to press the button, there would be no "brain wave spike," and the decision was therefore not made by the "material brain." So, Libet believed that if he had not proven there was "free will," then he had proven that people had "free won't."

Libet proved that God gave Adam and Eve a "free won't": If they had the will, they could have resisted the temptation.

"And the LORD God commanded the man, "You are free to eat from any tree in the garden; but you must not eat from the tree of the knowledge of good and evil, for when you eat from it you will certainly die." (Genesis 2: 16,17 NIV)

Finally, Dr. Egnor emphasized that in order to better understand the human brain and mind, it was best to explain them in terms of dualism. Dr. Egnor pointed out that if we think the natural world is purposeful and designed, then it is easier to understand.

In the nineteenth century, the German philosopher and psychologist Franz Brentano (1838–1917)[117] asked a very important question: "What is unique about the mind that makes it different from the matter?" His answer was: "The main difference is intentionality." Intentionality is the ability for something to be about something else. For example, when one thinks of Washington, DC, one thinks "about" a city. Only the mind has the ability to come up with an idea "about" something. No physical object has the ability to make a connection "about" anything. In a sense, intentionality reflects the grander "aboutness" of nature.

The magnificent part of this is teleology. Teleology is the tendency of a process in nature to go somewhere or become something. For example, an acorn growing on an oak tree is to become an oak tree. Unless we understand the purpose, we will not be able to understand the mind, or nature.

Dr. Egnor pointed out that Darwinian biologists try not to consider teleology, but if the purpose of each part (organ) of the organism is not involved, the biologist cannot explain the organism. It is impossible for a person to understand the heart unless understanding the purpose of the heart is pumping blood. Purpose is like intentionality or mind. Behind the implication is that behind the universe there is a grand mind, a mind that is reflected in a way that the universe works, and that is God. Everything in nature shows purpose, goal-directedness, teleology, and intentionality. It is a reflection of a much higher mind—God.

God-Given Life

Since ancient times, humans have regarded blood as the source of life. If we get sick and go to the hospital, the doctor's diagnosis is mostly based on the results of blood tests, because physiological changes and pathological changes in the organism usually cause changes in blood composition. This is what God meant when He said, "*the life of living creatures is in the blood.*"[118] Animals rely on blood circulation to survive, and from this blood circulation, we can see the amazing design of God.

The blood in the human body can circulate to every cell in the body, which is a miracle in itself. The vascular system that transports blood and the powerful heart are beyond human wisdom and design capabilities. Blood provides oxygen and nutrients to the body, and it helps the body remove metabolic waste. How to supply blood on time and on demand according to the needs of various tissue cells is also beyond human wisdom and ability.

If a person's heart beats seventy-five times per minute, on average, and that person's life span is seventy-eight years, his heart beats nearly 3.075 billion times in his life. Why is the heart so durable? It relies on its perfect design. For example, the muscle wall of the left ventricle is particularly thick because it needs to pump blood to systemic circulation. The right ventricle only pumps blood to the lungs, the distance is short, the blood pressure required is low, and the muscles do not need to be that thick. In addition, the heartbeat is regular, and myocardial rest (diastole) is much longer than work (systole).[119] This is also the reason why the heart is durable.

Do you know how long human blood vessels are? To allow the cells of the whole body to fully obtain oxygen and nutrients, blood vessels and capillaries branch all over the body. The total length of capillaries, arteries, and veins exceeds 100,000 kilometers, which is equivalent to the length of two and half circles around the earth.[120]

Human blood circulation is a perfect one-way flow, which is a superb and special design of God. The heart and all blood vessels are of "irreducible complexity design." Let us illustrate some of these points:

1. There are unidirectional valves, or check valves, between the heart chambers and between the atria and the connected blood vessels, allowing blood to flow in one direction only. There is a very thin and smooth endocardium on the inside of the heart to ensure smooth blood flow without turbulences.

Arteries are blood vessels that carry blood away from the heart. The arteries have no valves to ensure the smooth flow of blood. All veins have unidirectional valves, which open in the direction toward the heart. These valves are designed according to the location requirements of the blood vessels. Because the venous blood pressure is very low,[121] to allow the blood of the limbs to flow back to the heart under anti-gravity conditions, there are many one-way valves or check valves in all the veins of the limbs,[122] only allowing blood to flow upward, in a flow to the heart. At the same time, muscle exercise will put some pressure on the venous blood vessels and squeeze the blood in the blood vessels to flow upward. Just like when we squeeze a rubber hose filled with water, if the bottom is blocked, the water can only flow upward. It also proves that extremity exercise or massage is very important to promote the health of blood circulation.

2. Blood enters a tissue from small arteries into a network of capillaries that may contain millions of capillaries. After the blood sends nutrients and oxygen from the capillary network, and takes carbon dioxide and metabolic waste away, the blood will flow out of the venules[123] This process causes the blood in the capillaries to slowly change from bright red to dark red. One end of the capillary

network is connected to small arteries, and the other end is connected to small veins. The blood circulation is a perfect closed-loop circuit system.

God-Given Breath

Then the Lord God formed a man from the dust of the ground and breathed into his nostrils the breath of life, and the man became a living soul.

(Genesis 2:7 kJV)

God breathed into Adam's nostrils. On the one hand, this enabled Adam to breathe, and on the other hand, Adam was given a spirit to communicate with God. Because breathing is very important to human life, God has specially designed protections for the airway during swallowing, as shown in the following lines of defense, that prevent food from entering the trachea by mistake:[124]

1. When a person is swallowing, the uvula will automatically turn upward to close the nasal cavity, and the structural protection device, the epiglottis, at the top of the airway, will fold down to cover the glottis, which protects the airway.

2. Except for the first cartilage ring, which is a complete O-shaped cartilage ring, the trachea is supported by a string of incomplete C-shaped cartilage rings. The C-shaped gap faces the inner side and is closed with an elastic connective tissue layer. This design is such that when food enters the esophagus, the cartilage ring has the ability to locally stretch, to ensure the trachea is unobstructed.

The lungs[125] are also an "irreducible complexity" of design. The left lung is divided into two lobes, and the right lung is divided into three lobes, to avoid the spread of infection to the entire lung when one lobe is infected. After the trachea divides into left and right bronchi, it branches several times and finally divides into bronchioles. The entire tracheal distribution looks like an upside-down tree. All tracheal branches are distributed in a fractal pattern,[126] ensuring that air is distributed evenly to each lung cell.

The bronchioles are very thin, and at the end are individual alveoli, also called alveolar clusters, or air sacs.[127] The walls of the bronchioles are thin enough to facilitate gas exchange. The total internal surface area of the entire lung is about 140 square meters, forming a large surface area in the narrow space of the chest cavity. It is enough to meet the needs of people's strenuous exercise. This is a very amazing design and a wonderful design of God.

When a person breathes normally at rest, the chest cavity does not expand and contract much, providing about 25 percent of the total breathing volume; the dome muscle at the bottom of the chest cavity (i.e., the diaphragm) provides about 75 percent of the normal, resting, breathing volume.[128] Therefore, there is a possibility of suffocation if a heavy pressure put on top of the abdomen which causes the diaphragm not to be able to move. Deep breathing, that is, breathing in the abdominal cavity, provides the body with essential oxygen and promotes blood circulation. All God's designs are comprehensive considerations.

God-Given Energy with Enjoyment of Eating

God designed the human digestive system[129] to let people enjoy eating, convert food to their daily required energy, ingest nutrients to complete daily activities, and build new cells. It is a long, complex process beyond human wisdom. Both the structure and the process show the "irreducible complexity design" feature.

To design the system, God knew the structure and the properties of our daily foods. Our daily foods contain four kinds of biological molecules or macromolecules: the lipids, the carbohydrates, the proteins, and the nucleic acids. These molecules are long-chain polymers that need to be broken down into monomers (fatty acids, sugars, amino acids, and nucleotides acids) so they can be absorbed into the bloodstream to build cells in the body tissues.[130] The digestive system is an automatic food disassembly and processing line. The structure is comprised of eight organs: the mouth, throat, esophagus, stomach, small intestine, large intestine, rectum, and anus. In addition, the liver, gallbladder, and pancreas provide enzymes for chemical digestion at the right steps.

The first processing step is chewing, which uses the teeth to cut food into small pieces at the same time saliva is introduced to provide moisture, to turn food into bolus, making it easy to swallow, and enzymes in the saliva break down any starch. After swallowing the food into the esophagus, the transport of food is a cleverly designed involuntary mechanism called peristalsis, in which the smooth muscles of the walls of the digestive organs take turns contracting and relaxing to squeeze food through the lumen or cavity of the alimentary tract. Waves of peristalsis continue through the esophagus, the stomach, and the intestines

When foods enter the stomach, hormones, secreted by cells in the stomach lining, trigger the release of stomach gastric juice, which contains enzymes (pepsin) and acids (hydrochloric acid), plus some mucus and water. The key is the correct pH value (about 1) that only dissolves the food and breaks down its proteins, but that does not hurt the stomach wall, which is coated with mucus. Do scientists have the ability to design this?

In the next step, inside the small intestine, the liver sends bile to the gallbladder, which secretes this into the duodenum to dissolve fat. The enzymes break down fat to fatty acids and glycerol for easier absorption in later steps. The enzymes are also carrying out the final deconstruction of the proteins into amino acids and the carbohydrates into glucose. This happens in the small intestine's lower regions, the jejunum and ileum, which are coated in millions of tiny projections called villi. The design of the villi is also outside of human imagination. It has a huge surface area to maximize molecules' absorption and transference into the bloodstream. The blood carries the molecules to feed the body's organs and tissues. The leftover fiber and dead cells sloughed off during digestion makes its way into the large intestines (colon). The colon drains out most of the remaining fluids through the intestine wall, leaving a soft mass called the stool. The colon squeezes this by-product into a pouch called the rectum, where nerves sense its expansion, and tell the body when it's time to expel the wastes through the anus.

From the above brief description, there must be an intelligent designer knowing the human body's requirements and about edible foods to be able to design such efficient digesting system.

God's High-Efficiency Cleaning Design

The body's metabolism wastes were cleaned up by the liver, which plays a tremendous role in directing the dead cells and leftover chemicals to the digestive and urinary systems. The digestive system cleans out the solid waste, and the urinary system cleans out the chemical waste.[131]

The urinary system, especially the kidneys, conducts all sorts of important homeostatic tasks, like regulating body water volume, iron-salt concentrations, and pH levels, as well as influencing red blood cell production and blood pressure.

The kidneys[132] are high-efficiency filters. The average volume of the adult's kidneys is 146 cm³ (0.146 liters) on the left and 134 cm³ (0.134 liters) on the right. At any given moment, the kidneys hold 20 percent of the total blood volume, which means the kidneys filter 120 to 140 liters of blood every day. Therefore, the structure of the kidneys must be perfectly designed. The blood is removed from the kidneys first; then the kidneys take back the blood with nutrients and filters out the water into the bladder.

Another major function of the kidneys is to balance salt and water in the blood, which is processed in the tubes of the urinary system. Each kidney has three distinct layers, the outer most cortex, the medulla (a set of cone-shaped masses of tissue that secrete urine into tiny sac-like tubules), and finally the innermost layer is the renal pelvis, a funnel-shaped tube surrounded by smooth muscle that use peristalsis to move urine out of the kidney, into the ureter, and into the bladder. The structure of the kidney is also an "irreducible complex design.

God's Automatic Monitoring System

In an earlier section of this book, we discussed the nervous system, which uses lightning-fast electrochemical action potentials, delivered by an expressway made of neurons to specific cells and organs to protect the body. The human body also has an endocrine system that uses a slower, wider stream of chemical messengers (hormones) that travel through the bloodstream. They move more slowly but produce widespread effects that last longer than an action potential to maintain a homeostasis in the body functions. The two systems complement each other to protect and sustain human daily activities.

The hypothalamus is the connection between the brain (nervous system) and the endocrine system. Either system may take action or override the other system, depending on what kind of situation the body faces in that moment. A good example was given by Paul Andersen in his YouTube presentation,[133] as follows:

There is a nervous connection from the brain to the adrenal medulla, which secretes epinephrine. Epinephrine is a form of adrenaline. The adrenaline will distribute throughout the body to trigger the "fight or flight" response. So, if you almost get into a car accident, the nervous system will help you to not get into that accident. You will feel adrenaline coursing through your whole body. Your metabolism will speed up to suppress your digestive system, helping you to become more alert.

The endocrine system has three glands in the brain and seven glands in the body to produce over fifty hormones.[134] Each gland secretes one or more hormones into the blood stream. How can all fifty hormones find their own target receptor cells?

A hormone has its specific shape which needs special designed receptors in the target tissue cells to match the shape. We can regard the hormone as a key and the target receptor cell as a lock. When the key matches with the lock, then together they trigger the biochemical or physiological changes inside the cell. Who designed the fifty hormones and the matching receptor cells? When to secrete a specific hormone and how much to secrete are also big questions. For example, the growth hormone may start to secrete at very early stage of life and the amount secreted may be different at different stages of life span. A significant amount of sex hormones (testosterone or estrogen) may be secreted just before puberty. Who designed the amino acid-base water-soluble hormones or lipid soluble hormones like steroids to trigger the receptors on the cell surface or inside the target cells? *"God is love"* is expressed in the endocrine system.

God designed the pineal gland to secrete melatonin at nighttime, when people close their eyes to get a good night's sleep. This shows God designed the human body to rest in the evening and be able to work in the daytime. This also acts as an internal clock.

To protect us from serious inflammatory injury after an accident or injury, the adrenal cortex secretes glucocorticoids, which are anti-inflammatory. This also shows the love of God. In fact, every gland and its secreted hormones are purposely designed for the good of the human body. We will mention a few of these as follows:

The thyroid gland secretes T3 and T4 hormones, which regulate the body's metabolism. A hyperactive thyroid has a high metabolism, and a hypoactive thyroid will have a low metabolism. The thyroid gland also secretes calcitonin, which lowers the calcium level in the blood and turns it back into the bone. However, the human body requires a certain calcium level for proper function. To avoid the calcium concentration becoming too low, a parathyroid secretes a hormone that will take action when calcium in the blood is too low. Therefore, the calcium level in the blood is kept within a suitable range.

The surface of the pancreas contents beta cells and alpha cells that secrete insulin and glucagon. Insulin lowers the blood sugar (glucose) levels, and glucagon raises the blood sugar from glycogen in the liver.

Each and every gland and hormone is necessary for the health of the human body. Therefore, the endocrine system is an "irreducible complexity" designed system

God's Careful Protection

God designed the human body, providing all its organs with built-in protections, some already stated above. In this section, we will talk about the immune system,[135] which provides constant protection, and the sympathetic nervous system, which enables us to fight or escape from danger.

In our life spans, we face many bacterial and viral attacks. Fortunately, our body has a well-designed immune system to safeguard against infection, illness, and disease. This system is a vast network of cells, tissues, and organs that coordinate the human body's defenses against any threat to its health, whether bacterial, viral, or toxic.

Our bone marrow generates between four thousand and eleven thousand defensive white blood cells (leukocytes) in every microliter of blood. These white blood cells migrate into the bloodstream and the lymphatic system, a network of vessels that helps clear out body toxins and waste. Leukocytes are like security personnel, constantly screening the blood, tissues, and organs for suspicious signs of unhealthy. This system primarily relies on cues called antigens. These molecular traces on the surface of the pathogens and other foreign substances betray the presence of invaders. As soon as leukocytes detect them, it only takes minutes for the body's protective immune response to kick in. Threats to our bodies are hugely variable, so the immune response must be equally adaptable. That means relying on many types of leukocytes to tackle the responses in different ways. Despite this diversity, scientists classify leukocytes in two main cellular groups.

One group of leukocyte cells called T-cells go in search of infected body cells and swiftly kill them off. Meanwhile, B-cells and helper T-cells use the information gathered from unique antigens to start producing special proteins called antibodies. This is the piece of resistance: Each antigen has a unique, matching antibody that can latch on to it like a lock and key to destroy the invading cells. B-cells can produce millions of these, which then cycle through the body and attack the invaders until the worst of the threat is neutralized. While all this is going on, other familiar symptoms, like high temperature and swelling at the site of infection, are processes designed to aid the immune response. A warmer body makes it harder for bacteria and viruses to reproduce and spread, because they are temperature sensitive. When the body cells are damaged, they release chemicals that leak into the surrounding tissue, causing swelling, but this also attracts phagocytes, which consume the invaders and the damaged cells.

Usually, an immune response will eradicate a threat within a few days. This is not to stop the person from getting ill; that is not its purpose. Its actual job is to stop a threat from escalating to a dangerous level inside the body. Through constant surveillance over time, the immune system then provides another benefit: It helps us develop long-term immunity. When B-cells and T-cells identify antigens, they can use that information to recognize invaders in the future. So, when an invader revisits, the cells can swiftly deploy the right antibodies to tackle it before it affects any more cells. That is how you develop immunity to certain diseases, like the chickenpox.

The psalmist declared in Psalm 46:1: *"God is our refuge and strength, an ever-present help in trouble"* (NiV). This statement is often fulfilled when people face danger. When a person suddenly faces danger, his body often will exhibit an extraordinary ability to escape from that danger. When God designed the human body, He knew human beings might encounter dangers in life, so He gave people the ability to escape this danger in an emergency.

God designed the sympathetic nervous system and the autonomic nervous system as a balanced nervous system that enables the person to either fight or escape the danger; the parasympathetic nervous system is a resting, or normal, nervous system.[136]

Under the operation of the sympathetic nervous system, the heartbeat speeds up and increases the strength of the heart to contract, so it will increase the blood supply. At the same time, the coronary arteries expand, the breathing rate increases, the breathing becomes deeper, the breathing volume increases, and the bronchial passages expand. The renal arteries contract, and the kidney's blood supply is reduced; urine output is reduced to save water in the body. The blood supply to the gastrointestinal tract is reduced, and the gastrointestinal vasoconstriction is reduced. The liver will also release stored fat, turning it into energy. Peripheral vascular restriction reduces the blood supply to the surface of the body, and the skin may remain without blood supply for a long time, so more blood can be reserved for the vital organs. In case of injury while fleeing, there will be less bleeding. There will also be an increase in the amount of sweat and a cold sweat to prevent hyperthermia. When the danger has passed, the parasympathetic nervous system begins to work, and the human body gradually returns to normal.

Another of God's amazing designs gives the human body the ability to maintain homeostasis,[137] which is the necessary ability to survive in different environments.[138] God has set some parameters in the human body to maintain the stable operation of the internal system and keep the best function of the human system. For example, body temperature and body fluid balance are maintained within a certain preset limit (steady-state range). Other variables include the pH of the extracellular fluid; the concentrations of sodium, potassium, and calcium; and the blood sugar levels. Despite changes in the environment, diet, or activity level, the human body still needs the ability to adjust these variables. Each of these variables is controlled by one or more regulators, or constant mechanisms, in the body, working together to sustain life. Below, we discuss body temperature as an example.

In every cell of the human body, there are enzymes.[139] If the body temperature rises or falls, it will change the shape of the enzyme. These new shapes of the enzyme cannot promote the body's biochemical reactions. Therefore, it is very important to maintain a constant body temperature in the body.

A body temperature of 36.9°C is considered a normal body temperature (set point). When the body temperature becomes too cold, the temperature sensors in the body will tell the body to react. For example, blood flow into capillaries will be reduced, or even shaking in the body to generate heat will occur; in more serious cases, the body will produce more thyroid hormones to increase the metabolic rate. Conversely, when the temperature of the human body is too high, the capillaries will expand, and more hot blood will flow into the capillaries; the heat will be dissipated from the skin surface, and the blood will return to the body to cool it down; the human body will also produce sweat to dissipate the heat.

This chapter states that the design and creation of the human organs and the systems in the human body demonstrates the love of God. All the designs were made out of love, including suitable functions for people to enjoy life and protect themselves against danger. All these designs are of "irreducible complexity." Every organ and system have its purpose, and it is fully in line with the functions designed for individual purposes. Everyone has a unique design. The human body is a testament to God's design.

Scripture Meditation

For you created my inmost being;
you knit me together in my mother's womb.

   I praise you because I am fearfully and wonderfully made;
your works are wonderful,
I know that full well. (Psalm 139:13,14)

   The highest heavens belong to the LORD,
but the earth he has given to mankind. (Psalm 115:16)

   But it is the spirit in man,
the breath of the Almighty, that makes him understand. (Job 32:8)

   (Jesus say) *The Spirit gives life; the flesh counts for nothing. The words I have spoken to you—they are full of the Spirit and life.* (John 6:63)

Summary Remarks

Summarizing the main points discussed in the previous four chapters, I believe we can prove that all things in the universe were created by God, as stated in the Bible. This fact has been proven by many scientists over the last few centuries. Because the human eye has limited visibility, the ancients looked at the movement of the celestial bodies like "*blind men touching an elephant*". With the advancement of science and technology, astronomers now see that the universe and the number of galaxies is beyond human imagination. Science provides that the universe started with the Big Bang and continues to expand. Just as it states in the Bible, in Genesis 1:1 (NIV), it declares, "*In the beginning God created the heavens and the earth,*" demonstrating that the universe had its beginning at creation. The Big Bang is a "singularity" in science, and so far, scientists have been unable to create or even explain this singularity. All creations in the universe have a purpose: God created everything to demonstrate His love for mankind.

According to the Bible, as revealed by God, the plants and animals were first created in a fully grown, mature stage, "*according to their kinds.*" Many species of animals were created all at the same time (the Cambrian explosion). This indicates there was no need for evolution. All species were clearly defined at their initial creation. If they had not been created at the same time, after a few generations, there would have been an odd menagerie of species. The origin of life, then, becomes a "biological singularity"; current biologists have no ability to explain this singularity. God's creation is beyond human imagination and understanding.

The "biological singularity" was proven by an event in the history of Israel: the Rebellion of Korah. In this event, God performed a miracle to restore Moses and Aaron's authority to lead His people in Israel. In the miracle, "*Aaron's staff, which represented the tribe of Levi, had not only sprouted but had budded, blossomed and produced almonds*" (Numbers 17:8 NIV).

On the other hand, the theory of evolution is based on the observation of results in the appearance of differences in small animals found in different environments, called micro-evolution. Micro-evolution is an ability that was given by God to animals, enabling them to adapt to changes in their environment that they might ultimately multiply and fill the earth (Genesis 1:22). Darwin extended the ability of micro-evolution to an unseen ability of the macro-evolution – the capability of an ape evolving into Human. This is an excessive claim on the animal's biological evolutionary capability.

In Darwin's era, biological study was just being established. The optical microscope could not see the complex structure that exists inside each cell. Scientists did not realize the degree of complexity of the cell structure. They thought the structure was very simple, and thus, the formation of life was considered to be easy. Scientists later proved that organisms cannot perform "spontaneous generation." Where and how would they start to evolve? Recently, scientists concluded they cannot produce amino acids or proteins, let alone create life. Hence, nature itself cannot produce even the simplest form of life. So, where and how could the evolution process have begun? The simplest creatures do not have the ability to evolve to more complex creatures by themselves.

After the molecular structure of DNA was deciphered in 1953, scientists recognized that DNA is very similar to the digital-code program of a computer. It provides the information about the manufacture of life. The writing of a computer program requires a "programmer"; similarly, the creation of DNA requires a Creator. With the rapid progress in the study of modern microbiology, scientists have learned that the simplest organisms have the characteristics of "irreducible complexity," which means they could only have been designed by an "intelligent designer." This theory is called "the intelligent design theory." Atheistic evolution scholars attack "intelligent design theory" as unscientific. But the examples given by the atheists to attack this theory are even less scientific (see Chapter 3).

The "Irreducible Complexity" design feature was found in small organisms by the Intelligent Design scientist, Michael Behe, was discovered a long time ago by King Solomon, as he stated in Ecclesiastes 3:14: *I know that everything God does will endure forever; nothing can be added to it and nothing taken from it. God does it so that people will fear him*" (NIV). The statement that "nothing can be added to it and nothing taken from it" is, in fact, the "Irreducible Complexity" concept

The structure of the human body is very "fearfully and wonderfully made." It is of an "irreducible complexity" design. Its entire design is purposeful and rooted in love. Its design enables mankind to enjoy life while being protected. All the tissues, organs, and systems of the human body prove that only God could have designed it. This is the ultimate proof that the "God's creation" is the truth.

In summary, current scientific discoveries have shown that the "God's creation" is the truth. The "intelligent design" theory agrees with biology.

Biology is science. The macro- evolution theory was not base on scientific findings is neither science nor truth.

Scripture Meditation

"Do not let your hearts be troubled. You believe in God; believe also in me. My Father's house has many rooms; if that were not so, would I have told you that I am going there to prepare a place for you? And if I go and prepare a place for you, I will come back and take you to be with me that you also may be where I am. **(John 14:1-3)**

[Jesus said,] "I came from the Father and entered the world; now I am leaving the world and going back to the Father." (John 16:28)

. And this is the testimony: God has given us eternal life, and this life is in his Son. Whoever has the Son has life; whoever does not have the Son of God does not have life (1 John 5:11,12)

Yet to all who did receive him, to those who believed in his name, he gave the right to become children of God—children born not of natural descent, nor of human decision or a husband's will, but born of God. (john 1:12,13)

Appendix 1

Trinity God

The Trinity is a basic Christian doctrine.[140] It defines God as being one God, existing in three coequal, coeternal, and consubstantial divine persons: God the Father (YHWH), God the Son (Jesus Christ), and God the Holy Spirit—three distinct Persons sharing one essence. In this context, the three divine Persons define who God is, while the one essence defines what God is. This expresses, at the same time, their distinction and their indissoluble unity. Thus, the whole work of creation and grace is seen as a single common operation of all three divine Persons, in which each manifest what is proper to it in the Trinity, so that all things are "from the Father," "through the Son," and "in the Holy Spirit." This relationship was clearly shown in the "Shield of the Trinity" in Figure 1.[141]

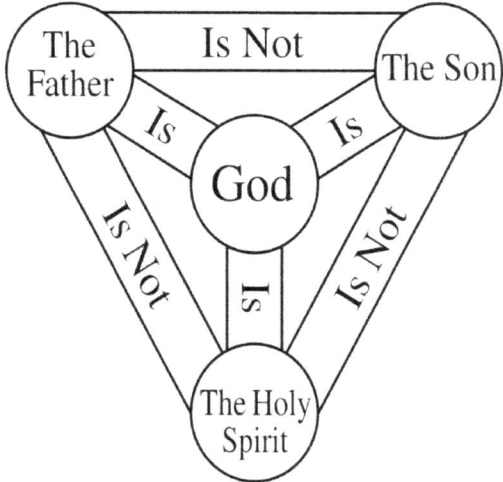

Figure 1: A compact diagram of the Trinity is known as the "Shield of Trinity."

The Shield is not generally intended to be a schematic diagram of the structure of God, but it presents a series of statements about the correlation between the Persons of the Trinity.

The Bible does not have a name for the "Triune God," but from the revelation of the contents of the Bible, we can clearly see that God is the "Triune God." The details of the biblical explanation are beyond the scope of this appendix. We will give a scientific analogy to let the readers know how the "Triune God" can exist.

The concept of the Trinity is very difficult to explain because there is no such entity elsewhere in the world. A person is an individual with a body, and two people cannot be combined into one person. God is an invisible Spirit.[142] The best way to understand the invisible "God" is to describe it or explain it by an analogy. When Jesus Christ explained the Holy Spirit to Nicodemus, a Pharisee of the Jews, He used the analogy of the wind as an example.

[Jesus answered,] "The wind blows wherever it pleases. You hear its sound, but you cannot tell where it comes from or where it is going. So it is with everyone born of the Spirit." (John 3:8 NIV)

We cannot see the wind, but we can see the effects of the wind, such as the sound of the wind causing the leaves to flutter. The sound of the wind is produced by invisible soundwaves. When there is treble, midrange, and bass sounds together at the same time, they are as a single sound, one that contains three scales of high, medium, and low, so the soundwave can be three in one.

In the same way, some electromagnetic waves in the universe[143] are other invisible waves that can be felt by people. Here we will use electromagnetic waves as an analogy referring to God. Another reason we use this analogy is that there are several verses in the Bible that refer to Jesus' appearances as light. In the book of Acts, when Saul was on the way to Damascus, Jesus appeared to him as a strong, bright light (Acts 9:3 NIV)

As he [Saul] neared Damascus on his journey, suddenly a light from heaven flashed around him.

In the book of Revelation, the apostle John saw the city of the New Jerusalem in this way:

The city does not need the sun or the moon to shine on it, for the glory of God gives it light, and the Lamb is its lamp. (Revelation 21:23 NIV)

"*The glory of God gives it light. . . .*" Light is an electromagnetic wave. God Himself is definitely not an electromagnetic wave. If we think of God as infinite energy, He will emit an electromagnetic wave. Electromagnetic waves have different wavelengths, or different frequencies. The greater the energy of an electromagnetic wave, the smaller the wavelength, and the greater the frequency. The true God has infinite energy and infinite glory; therefore, the true God has infinite frequency and an infinitely small wavelength. In physics, the wavelength is expressed as a vector,[144] and an infinitesimal vector should have no length, but we give it an arbitrary length for an easier explanation. Three equal-length vectors in the clockwise direction represent the three "divine Persons" of the Trinity, which form an equilateral triangle (see Figure 2).

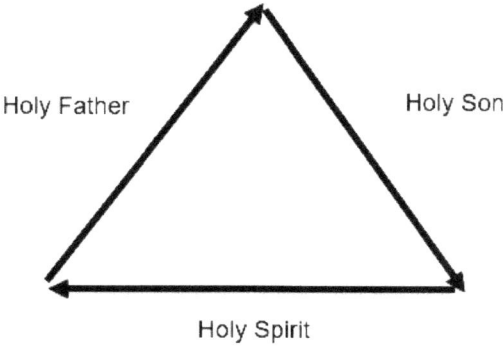

Figure 2. Using electromagnetic wave vectors as an analogy for the Trinity

The three vectors in Figure 2 represent the three divine persons of the trinity. The vector which starts from the left bottom to the top represents the Holy Father God, the vector from the top to the right bottom represents the Holy Son, and the vector from the right to the left represents the Holy Spirit. From the point of view of electromagnetics, the combined energy intensity, of the three vectors, is perpendicular to the plane formed by the three vectors, and the three electromagnetic waves combined together form a combined electromagnetic wave, which is analogous to the "Trinity" God. Moreover, the product of three infinite (∞) energies is infinite (∞); whether they are added together or multiplied, as in the following simple formula:

$$\infty + \infty + \infty = \infty$$

$$\infty \times \infty \times \infty = \infty$$

Infinity is also analogous to the power of God. The "Trinity" nature of the true God is complete, flawless, and holy, without impurity. Therefore, the Father, the Son, and the Holy Spirit are each completely holy. Only individual holiness can be combined to remain God's complete holiness. Three divine Gods glorify each other among the "Trinity." The true God is agape love.[145] This is the perfect love among them, and it extends to fill the whole universe and last forever.

Scripture Meditation

[Jesus said,] "If you love me, keep my commands. And I will ask the Father, and he will give you another advocate to help you and be with you forever— the Spirit of truth. The world cannot accept him, because it neither sees him nor knows him. But you know him, for he lives with you and will be in you. I will not leave you as orphans; I will come to you. Before long, the world will not see me anymore, but you will see me. Because I live, you also will live. On that day you will realize that I am in my Father, and you are in me, and I am in you. Whoever has my commands and keeps them is the one who loves me. The one who loves me will be loved by my Father, and I too will love them and show myself to them."(John 14:15-21 NIV)

Appendix 2

The Physical Revelation
of The Cross

Genesis Chapter 3 stated the process and consequences of Adam and Eve's sin. God's right to govern the earth which he gave to Adam in the beginning; Adam has now passed this right of management to Satan through his sin. The most severe consequence was God's spirit left them and they became mortal. God wants to realize the purpose of having man with Him forever, Immediately God put forth a salvation plan for humans as stated in Genesis 3:15; (So the LORD God said to the serpent): *"15 And I will put enmity between you and the woman, and between your offspring and hers; he will crush your head, and you will strike his heel."*

This verse pointed out that Jesus will go to the cross to redeem the sins of mankind and defeat Satan (death), so that those who believe in Jesus can become children of God (John 1:12), and can restore the perfect cross relationship between God and man, and man to man.

This salvation plan was prophetic throughout the Old Testament and by Jesus Christ himself, as stated in Hebrew 1:1-2: *"In the past God spoke to our ancestors through the prophets at many times and in various ways, but in these last days he has spoken to us by his Son, whom he appointed heir of all things, and through whom also he made the universe."*

In this appendix, we will point out how the physical revelation of the cross in the Tabernacle and the camping arrangement of the Israelites reveal the salvation of Jesus Christ – the cross.

The Tabernacle reveals the redemption of Jesus Christ through the cross

In Exodus 25–31 and 35–40, the Bible describes how God instructed Moses in the detail of the construction of the Tabernacle and its contents. This was the portable earthly dwelling place of God. It was also the worship center of the Israelites from the time of the Exodus until the conquest of Canaan. Moses was instructed at Mount Sinai to construct and transport the Tabernacle for the Israelites in the wilderness of Mount Sinai. The

Tabernacle was completed by Moses according to God's instructions, with its entrance facing east. Its plan view diagram is shown in Figure 1.

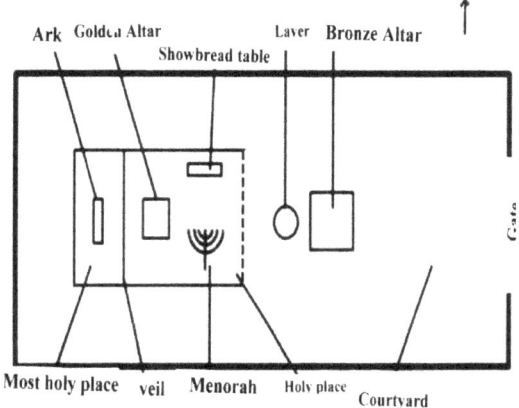

Figure 1. Plan view of the Tabernacle of the Israelites

As seen in Figure 1, when a priest entered the Tabernacle through the east gate, he would enter the (outer) courtyard, and there he would see the Bronze Altar and the Laver. He needed to wash his hands and feet before he entered the gate into the inner courtyard. The priest again washed his hands and feet before entering the Holy Place. Inside the Holy Place, there was a table with showbread on top on the right side of the table, and in the same distance on the left side stood the Golden Lampstand with seven oil lamps. In the center, closer to the veil, was the Golden Altar of Incense. Behind the veil was the Holy of Holies. The Ark of the Covenant was inside the Holy of Holies.

Referring to Figure 1 again, if one were facing west, from the Bronze Altar, to the Laver in the courtyard, to the Altar of Incense in the Holy Place, and then to the Ark of the Covenant in the Holy of Holies—together these form a vertical straight line; and the Golden Lampstand and the table of showbread in the Holy Place together form a horizontal line. The two lines are in the shape of, and become a symbol of, the cross.

The Camp of Israel Reveals the Salvation of Jesus Christ through the Cross

In the last section, the arrangement of the holy articles in the sanctuary revealed the salvation of Jesus Christ through the cross. In this section, we will show that the "camp of Israel" reveals the salvation of Jesus Christ through the cross.

In this section, I refer to an article by Chuck Missler.[146] His conclusion about the arrangement of the camp of Isreal was as follows:

It would appear to us that it is a cross! Isn't that remarkable? And this is from the Torah, not the New Testament! The New Testament is in the Old Testament concealed; the Old Testament is in the New Testament revealed. Isn't the Word of God fabulous?

In the center of the camp was the Tabernacle. It was surrounded by three Levite clans, as stated in Numbers 1:53 (NIV):

"The Levites, however, are to set up their tents around the tabernacle of the covenant law so that my wrath will not fall on the Israelite community. The Levites are to be responsible for the care of the tabernacle of the covenant law."

Levi had three sons—Gershon, Kohath, and Merari— who became the three Levite clans. The number of each clan (including males one month old and older) and their camping location were as follows:

The number of the Gershonite clans was 7,500, and they were to camp on the west, behind the Tabernacle. The number of the Kohathites was 8,600, and they were to camp on the south side of the Tabernacle. The number of the Merarite clans was 6,200, and they were to camp on the north side of the Tabernacle

Moses and Aaron and his sons were to camp to the east of the Tabernacle, toward the sunrise, in front of the tent of meeting.[147] They were responsible for the care of the sanctuary on behalf of the Israelites.

Next, the camping positions of the other twelve tribes were surrounding and farther away from the tent of meeting (the Tabernacle), according to God's command as stated in Numbers 2. The detail of their numbers and positions are described in Table 1.

Table 1 The Number of Israelites in each Tribe

Tribe's Name	Number	Division Total	Location
Camp of Ruben (Man)			
Ruben	46,500		
Simeon	59,300		
Gad	45,600	151,400	South
Camp of Judah (Lion)			
Judah	74,600		
Issachar	54,400		
Zebulun	57,400	186,400	East
Camp of Dan (Eagle)			
Dan	62,700		
Asher	41,500		
Naphtali	53,400	157,600	North
Camp of Ephraim (Ox)			
Ephraim	40,500		
Manasseh	32,200		
Benjamin	35,400	108,100	West
Total Israelites		603,500	

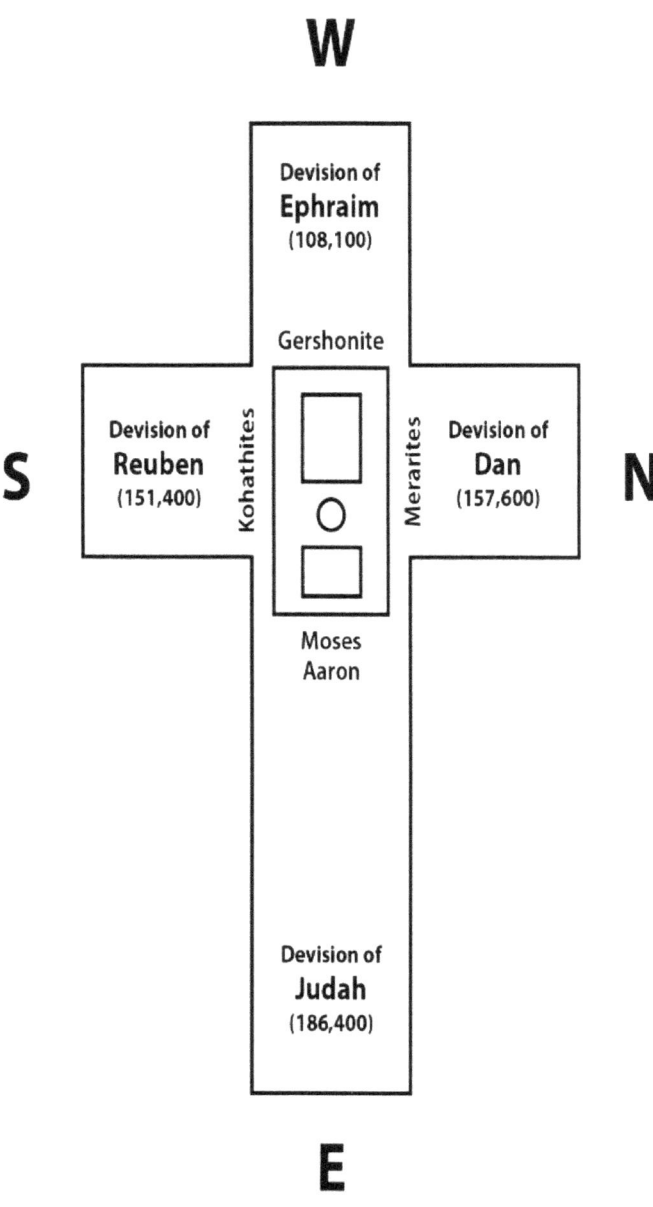

Figure 2. The Camp of Israelites

There were 186,400 males over twenty years old in the east; 108,100 in the west' 151,400 in the south; and 157,600 in the north. If this is sketched out according to the proportion of the number of people, the result is the shape of a cross, as shown in Figure 2. The west is oriented to the top of the drawing. The south and the north extend to almost the same distance. The ratio of the east and the west is 186,400/108,100, equal to 1.72433. This ratio is close to the golden ratio (φ=1.61803398875) we discussed in Chapter 4. This arrangement indicates that God was involved in the creation of all the Israelite people.

This was obviously God's formation, as revealed in the shape of the cross. Ancient and modern armies always camp in a square, rectangular, or circular shape. None of them have ever camped in the shape of the cross—except these early Israelites. When God was with them, the Israelites fought victoriously, and the sign of the cross was also a sign of victory and of glory. We know from the history of Israel that when God was with them, every war was won, even when just a few men were fighting.

Numbers 22–24 describes the story of Balak, the king of Moab, who summoned Balaam to Moab to put a curse on the Israelites. Three times Balaam tried to curse the Israelites, but each time God turned the curse into a blessing for the Israe*lites. The reason for this was pointed out by Moses in Deuteronomy 23:5 (NIV): "However, the Lord your God would not listen to Balaam but turned the curse into a blessing for you, because the Lord your God loves yo*u."

The arrangement of putting the Tabernacle in the center of the camp shows what God's intention was: "*I will dwell among the people of Israel and will be their God*"(Exodus 29:45 ESV). The cross is the symbol of His salvation and His love. Being under the cross is the same as being in Christ, gaining all His protection.

When Balaam stood at three different high grounds looking at a partial portion of the Israelites camping array, he saw how the lineup exhibited the shape of a cross. Balaam was amazed by the beauty of the lineup, and all he could do was praise it and pronounce a blessing upon it.

The veil in the Temple separates the Holy Place from the Holy of Holies. The Holy of Holies is the "dwelling place" of God. Only the high priest could enter once a year with the atonement of the blood of cattle and sheep. But Christ offered an eternal sacrifice for sin when Jesus, on the cross, said, "I*t is finished.*"[148] "At that moment the curtain (veil) of the temple was torn in two from top to bottom" (Matthew 27:51 NIV). This meant the redemption of Jesus Christ had torn down the barrier between God and sinful men. The promise of God was fulfilled: "*For God so loved the world that he gave his one and only Son, that whoever believes in him shall not perish but have eternal life*" (John 3:16 NIV)

John 1:43–51, in which Jesus called Philip and Nathanael, describes the process of salvation at the cross. In the last two verses of this passage, Jesus Christ said this to Nathanael:

Jesus said, "You believe because I told you I saw you under the fig tree. You will see greater things than that." He then added, "Very truly I tell you, you will see heaven open, and the angels of God ascending and descending on the Son of Man." —John 1:50–51 MIV

In the last verse of this passage, Jesus told Nathanael that He was the "heavenly ladder" in Jacob's dream at Bethel, as described in Genesis 28:10–21. Therefore, the veil also represented the body of Jesus.[149]

From the above argument, the Ladder foreshadowed the body of Jesus, and the sanctuary did as well. At the very moment of Jesus' death on the cross, the veil in the Temple was torn into two from top to bottom, and the Spirit of God returned to heaven. We can regard Jesus (the sanctuary) thus: [He] "stood up between the heaven and earth. Jesus is the entire cross." He opened His hands facing the east and called all people in the world to follow Him. Holding the showbread in His left hand, He said: "*I am the bread of life. Whoever comes to me will never go hungry; and whoever believes in me will never be thirsty*" (John 6:35 NIV). Holding the Golden Lampstand in His right hand, He said: "*I am the light of the world. Whoever follows me will never walk in darkness, but will have the light of life*" (John 8:12 NIV). He also declared thus: "*I am the way and the truth and the life*" (John 14:6 d). Now, as long as those who believe Jesus is the Savior come to Him to repent and be baptized, they will become new creations (see 2 Corinthians 5:17), and citizens of the kingdom of heaven.

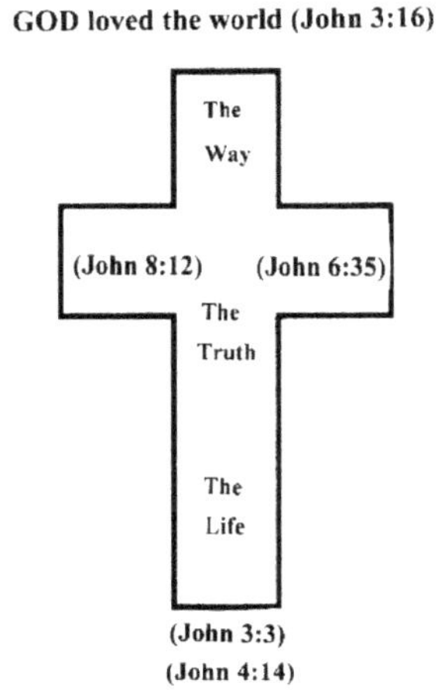

GOD loved the world (John 3:16)

The
Way

(John 8:12)   (John 6:35)
The
Truth

The
Life

(John 3:3)
(John 4:14)

Figure 3 The body of Jesus Christ is the heavenly laddler

Scripture Meditation

[5] *In your relationships with one another,*
have the same mindset as Christ Jesus:

[6] *Who, being in very nature[a]* God,
   did not consider equality with God something
to be used to his own advantage;
[7] *rather, he made himself nothing*
   by taking the very nature[b] of a servant,
   being made in human likeness.
[8] *And being found in appearance as a man,*
   he humbled himself
   by becoming obedient to death—
      even death on a cross!
[9] *Therefore God exalted him to the highest place*
   and gave him the name that is above every name,
[10] *that at the name of Jesus every knee should bow,*
   in heaven and on earth and under the earth,
[11] *and every tongue acknowledge that Jesus Christ is Lord,*
   to the glory of God the Father.
   (Philippians 2: 5 -11 NIV)

Endnotes

1. See https://en.wikipedia.org.wiki.truth, "truth."

2. See https://en.wikipedia.org.widi.Laozi, "Laozi."

3. See https://en.wikipedia.org.wiki.TaoTeChing, "Tao Te Ching."

4. See Lîm Gí-tông (Chinese 林语堂) at https://zh-min- nan. wikipedia. org.wiki; 道德经 林语堂英文版 1-31 章_ Monica_ 新浪博客; http://blog. sina.com. cn

5. See https://en.wikipedia.org.wiki.DavidPawson, "David Pawson."

6. David Pawson, "Unlocking the Bible," Bible study series, John 1–2.

7. See https://en.wikipedia.org.wiki.majorreligiousgroups, "major religious groups."

8. *"For since the creation of the world God's invisible qualities— his eternal power and divine nature—have been clearly seen, being understood from what has been made, so that people are without excus*e" (Romans 1:20 NIV).

9. See http://en.wikipedia.org.wiki.intelligentdesign, "intelligent design.

10. See http://en.wikipedia.org.wiki.originalsin, "original sin.

11. *"In the past God spoke to our ancestors through the prophets at many times and in various ways"* (Hebrews 1:1 NIV).

12. *"By faith we understand that the universe was formed at God's command, so that what is seen was not made out of what was visible"* (Hebrews 11:3 NIV)

13. And God said, *"Let there be lights in the vault of the sky to separate the day from the night, and let them serve as signs to mark sacred times, and days and year*s" (Genesis 1:14 NIV).

14. Parallax is a daily experience. When a person moves from one point to another, the distant background does not move, but objects at close range seem to move. The closer the object moves, the greater the distance relative to the background. This movement, the distance is the parallax. Astronomers use the parallax caused by the earth's rotation, revolution, or different positions formed by different observatories to measure the distance between nearby stars. This method cannot accurately measure the distance of more distant stars.

15. Due to the improvement in telescopes, the latest estimate is two million light-years. In astronomy, the distance is calculated in light-years. One light- year is equivalent to the one-year journey of light in a vacuum, which is equal to 9,460,000,000,000 (9.46×10^{12}) kilometers. If a galaxy is one hundred million light- years away from the earth, when we observe it, we are seeing the light that it produced one hundred million years ago. The farther a galaxy is from the earth, the earlier in time the galaxy was formed.

16. See https://en.wikipedia.org/wiki/Dark_matter, "dark matter."

17. See https://en.wikipedia.org.wiki.steady-statemodel, "steady-state model."

18. *"By faith we understand that the universe was formed at God's command, so that what is seen was not made out of what was visible"* (Hebrews 11:3 NIV).

19. Stephen W. Hawking and Roger Penrose, "The Singularities of Gravitational Collapse and Cosmology," proceedings of The Royal Society of London A 314: 529-548 (1970); S.W. Hawking, *A Brief History of Time: From the Big Bang to Black Holes* (Toronto: Bantam Books, 1988). Also known as: The Penrose–Hawking singularity theorems.

20. Stephen Hawking, L. Mlodinow, The Grand Design, 2010. 大設計 郭兆林和周念縈譯 (Writers House, 2011).

21. Hugh Ross, *The Fingerprint of God* (Orange, CA: Promise, 1989), 129.

22. See https://en.wikipedia.org.wiki.ageofearth, "age of earth."

23. C.S. Lewis, *Mere Christianity* (New York: McMillan Publishing, 1952).

24. 1. *"God saw that the light was good"* (Genesis1:4 NIV); 2. After He made the land and sea, *"God saw that it was good"* (Genesis 1:10

NIV); 3. After He created vegetation on the land, *"God saw that it was good"* (Genesis 1:12 NIV); 4. God set the sun, moon, and stars in the vault of the sky, and *"God saw that it was good"* (Genesis 1:18 NIV); 5. After God created fishes and birds, *"God saw that it was good"* (Genesis 1:21 NIV); 6. *"God made the wild animals . . . the livestock . . . and all the creatures that move along the ground. And God saw that it was good"* (Genesis 1:25 NIV).

25. *"So God created mankind in his own image, in the image of God he created them; male and female he created them"* (Genesis 1:27 NIV).

26. Spencer Wells, *The Journey of Man: A Genetic Odyssey* (Princeton: Princeton University Press, 2002).

27. See imagehttps://en.wikipedia.org.wiki.primordialsoup, "primordial soup."

28. Stanley Miller, "A Production of Amino Acids Under Possible Primitive Earth Conditions," Science, vol. 117, 1953: 528–29.

29. Because amino acids are the basic units that make up proteins, amino acids have chiral properties, and there are two structural types: D-type and L- type. Natural amino acids are L-type. The synthetic amino acids D-type and L-type each account for 50 percent, and there is no way for people to synthesize 100 percent pure L-type amino acids

30. J. D. Watson and F.H.C. Crick, "Molecular structure of nucleic acids: A structure for deoxyribose nucleic acid," Nature, April (1953)

31. F. S. Collins, *Language of God* (New York: Free Press, 2006).

32. Watson and Crick, "Molecular structure of nucleic acids."

33. R. Pollack, *Signs of Life: The Language and Meanings of DNA* (New York: Houghton Mifflin, 1994).

34. See YouTube, "DNA Molecular Biology Visualizations— Wrapping and Replication."

35. W.K. Purves, D. Sadava, G.H. Orians, H.C. Heller, Life: The Science of Biology, 6th edition (Sunderland, MA: Sinsuer Association, 2001).

36. 邱恆德 (H.D Chiou), 神造的微米化工廠 ——細胞 傳 揚福音雜誌, May 2013., http://www.efccc.org// ArticleDetail.aspx?DocID=4016.

37. In the DNA, each segment becomes a gene. These genes contain instructions for making proteins. When a gene is turned on, an RNA polymerase attaches to the beginning of the gene. It moves along the DNA and forms a bunch of messenger RNA from free bases in the nucleus. The DNA code determines the order in which free bases are added to the mRNA. This process is called transcription.

38. Natural history is the budding period of the modern branch of science, which scientists study through the continuous observation, recording, and analysis of various creatures (animals, plants, fungi, microorganisms, etc.) on the earth and various things in their surrounding living environment.

39. The word protoplasm comes from the Greek word protos meaning "first" and the suffix plasm means "formed substance." In 1839, J.E. Purkinje (1787–1869) used it to represent substances in animal embryos. Later, in 1846, Hugo von Mohl (1805–1872) redefined the term to refer to "semi-fluid" substances within the plant cells. In 1869, Huxley called it the "physical basis of life" and believed that the properties of life were due to the distribution of molecules in this matter. See https:// en.wikipedia.org.wiki.protoplasm, "protoplasm."

40. The Greek philosopher Aristotle (384–322 BC) was one of the first scholars to record the theory of spontaneous generation and believed that life could come from non-living matter. Aristotle proposed that if living matter contained pneuma ("vital heat"), living things would be produced. An example is the sudden appearance of small organisms in a new puddle.

41. See https://en.wikipedia.ort.wiki.LouisPasteur, "Louis Pasteur."

42. J.D. Watson and F.H.C. Crick, "Molecular structure of nucleic acids: A structure for deoxyribose nucleic acid," *Nature*, April 1953.

43. Charles Darwin, *The Origin of Species by Means of Natural Selection* (London: John Murray, 1859).

44. Charles Darwin, *The Descent of Man;* see https://books. google.com. books.TheDescentofMan.

45. Darwin graduated from Cambridge University in England in 1831. He took part in the voyage of the H.H.S. Beagle because of his love of natural history and his desire to study biological life on the South American coast and in the Pacific islands. He took a five-year journey to these places

46. See https://en.wikipedia.org.wiki.microevolution, "microevolution."

47. See https://en.wikipedia.org.wiki.macroevolution, "macroevolution."

48. See https://en.wikipedia.org.wiki.mutation, "mutation."

49. See en.wikipedia.org.wiki.HugodeVries, "Hugo de Vries."

50. See en.wikipedia.org.wiki.ThomasHunt, "Thomas Hunt Morgan."

51. Sickle cell disease (SCD) is a group of inherited red blood cell deforming disorders. In SCD, red blood cells become hard and sticky, and they stick together, blocking blood flow. It is named for the deformed red blood cells that look like "scythes."

52. Luke W. Huang (MD 1942–) is a pediatrician in Los Angeles.

53. Luke W. Huang, "Science and Religion," Sunday school notes of EFC of Los Angeles, 2013 (written in Chinese).

54. See https://en.wikipedia.org.wiki.Downsyndrome, "Down syndrome."

55. See https://en.wikipedia.org.wiki.Patausyndrome, "Patau syndrome."

56. See https://en.wikipedia.org.wiki.Turnersyndrome, "Turner syndrome."

57. See https://en.wikipedia.org.wiki.Klinefeltersyndrome, "Klinefelter syndrome."

58. Darwin, The Origin of Species, p. 143.

59. Rachel Adams, "Be Grateful for the Intelligent Design of Your Eyes," YouTube, 2017.

60. See https://en.wikipedia.org.wiki.Cambrianexplosion, "Cambrian explosion.

61. See https://en.wikipedia.org.wiki.Natural_Theology_or_ Evidences, "Natural Theology or Evidences…"

62. Ibid.

63. Norman L. Geisler, Ph.D., *The Encyclopedia of Christian Apologetics* (Minneapolis: Baker Books, 1999), 574.

64. Richard Dawkins, *The Blind Watchmaker* (New York: Norton & Company, Inc., 1986).

65. Michael J. Behe, *Darwin's Black Box: The Biochemical Challenge to Evolution* (New York: Tree Press, 1996).

66. Michael Behe and Lee Strobel, "Molecular Machines Disprove Evolution," *Revolutionary: Michael Behe and the Mystery of Molecular Machines,* YouTube, 2017; see https:// en.wikipedia.crg. wiki.flagellum, "flagellum."

67. "Richard Dawkins Proves Intelligent Design in Five Minutes," YouTube, 2016.

68. Stephen C. Meyer, *Signature in the Cell: DNA and the Evidence for Intelligent Design* (San Francisco: HarperOne, 2009).

69. *A Most Important Discovery: Letters of Note, found at* https:// lettersofnote.com, July 10, 2015.

70. See https://en.wikipedia.org.wiki.sequencehypothesis, "sequence hypothesis."

71. CAD CAM refers to Computer-Assisted Design and Manufacture.

72. For a given protein, the arrangement of all the amino acids has a specific position sequence.

73. Meyer, Signature in the Cell.

74. Darwin's method was based on the method laid out by Charles Lyell (1797–1875) *in Principles of Geology:* "Being an attempt to explain the former changes of earth's surface by reference to causes now in operation."

75. *Signature in the Cell*: Stephen Meyer Faces His Critics, Part 1, YouTube.

76. Michael J. Behe, *Darwin Devolves: The New Science About DNA That Challenges Evolution* (San Francisco: HarperOne, 2019).

77. Stephen C. Myer, *Darwin's Doubt* (San Francisco: HarperOne, 2013).

78. Phyla is a level in the taxonomy ranking of organisms, located below the Kingdom and the class; sometimes it is also divided into subdivisions under the phylum. There are currently thirty-four phyla present in the animal kingdom.

79. Murry Edon, "Mathematical Challenges to Neo- Darwinism Conference," 1966.

80. Douglas Axe, Undeniable: How Biology Confirms Our Intuition That Life Is Designed (San Francisco: Harper One, 2017); Douglas D. Axe, "Estimating the Prevalence of Protein Sequences Adopting Functional Enzyme Folds," Journal of Molecular Biology, 2004.

81. See https://en.wikipedia.org.wiki.EricHDavidson, "Eric H. Davidson."

82. 史村志夫 (Fumio Shimura), "Einstein's Words for Your Life," 遠足文化,, 2016 (in Chinese).

83. John T. Scopes, a substitute teacher of physical education and science, had not taught the theory of evolution before.

84. See https://en.wikipedia.org.wiki.Scopestrial, "Scopes trial."

85. NOVA, "Judgment Day: Intelligent Design on Trial (creationism vs evolution)," YouTube, 2011.

86. See https://en.wikipedia.org.wiki.Tiktaalik, "Tiktaalik."

87. Bacterial type III secretion system: simple, needle- like complexes formed by proteins are used to inject toxins into the host organism. See https://en.wikipedia.org.wiki. type three secretion system, "type three secretion system." The function of the bacterial type III secretion system is completely different from that of the bacterial flagella, and the structure of the bacterial type III secretion system is also much simpler.

88. "Bacterial Flagella: A Paradigm for Design," YouTube, 2011.

89. See https://en.wikipedia.org.wiki.Chromosome2, "Chromosome 2."

90. Qin Shi Huang (Chinese: 秦始皇; lit. 'First Emperor of Qin,' 259–210), see https://en.wikipedia.org.wiki.Qin Shi Huang, "Qin Shi Huang."

91. Human Body 101 | National Geographic, YouTube, 2017.

92. See https://en.wikipedia.org.wiki.goldenratio, "golden ratio."

93. See https://en.wikipedia.org.wiki.MonaLisa, "Mona Lisa."

94. The posterior chamber is behind the iris and in front of the lens. The anterior chamber is between the iris and the cornea.

95. One of the causes of glaucoma is when the intraocular pressure is too high, which damages the optic nerves. One reason for high intraocular pressure can be when macular degeneration is treated with injections.

If the doctor does not check the intraocular pressure after the injection, the intraocular pressure can be well exceeded the normal range. The author received many injections for treatment of macular degeneration. Without the tests, my intraocular pressure had been exceeded. This caused the author's glaucoma which is believed to be a result of the malpractice of Dr. K., who specializes in the treatment of macular degeneration.

96. See https://en.wikipedia.org.wiki.taste, "taste."

97. John Campbell, Skin 5: Sensory Nerves, YouTube, 2014.

98. See https://en.wikipedia.org.wiki.vitaminD, "vitamin D."

99. *The Skeletal System: Crash Course A&P #19*, YouTube, 2015.

100. See https://en.wikipedia.org.wiki. hematopoietic stem cell, "hematopoietic stem cell."

101. Joints: Crash Course A&P #20, YouTube, 2015.

102. See https://en.wikipedia.org.wiki. human musculoskeletal system, "human musculoskeletal system"; Muscles, Part 1: Muscle Cells, Crash Course A&P #21, YouTube, 2015.

103. See https://en.wikipedia.org.wiki.nervoussystem, "nervous system."

104. Dr. Matt and Dr. Mike, "Blood Brain Barrier," YouTube; see https://en.wikipedia.org.wiki.bloodbrainbarrier, "blood-brain barrier."

105. Ibid.

106. See https://en.wikipedia.org.wiki.nervoussystem, "nervous system."

107. Dr. John Campbell, *Nervous System 1: Motor Neuron*, YouTube; Dr. John Campbell, Nervous System 2: Sensory Neuron, YouTube.

108. Ibid.

109. The first person to propose materialism was Democritus (460–370 BC). He believed that the things that exist in the world can be reduced to atoms and voids, and the behaviorists in the early twentieth century believed that only the behavior of a human being was important, not a person's mind. In the 1960s and 1970s, materialism regarded the brain to be the same as mind. There was no scientific basis for this conclusion.

110. See https://en.wikipedia.org.wiki.MichaelEgnor, "Michael Egnor."

111. Dr. Michael Egnor, *The Evidence against Materialism*, YouTube, 2019.

112. See https://en.wikipedia.org.wiki.corpuscallosum, "corpus callosum.

113. See https://en.wikipedia.org.wiki.WilderPenfield, "Wilder Penfield."

114. See https://en.wikipedia.org.wiki.AdrianOwen, "Adrian Owen."

115. A.M. Owen, M.R. Coleman, M.H. Davis, M. Boly, S. Laureys, and J.D. Pickard, "Detecting awareness in the vegetative state," Science, 313, 1402 (2006).

116. See https://en.wikipedia.org.wiki.BenjaminLibet, "Benjamin Libet."

117. See https://en.wikipedia.org.wiki.FranzBrentano, "Franz Brentano."

118. "*For the life of a creature is in the blood, and I have given it to you to make atonement for yourselves on the altar; it is the blood that makes atonement for one's life*" (Leviticus 17:11 NIV).

119. If the heart rate is seventy-five beats per minute, then the elapsed time to complete a cardiac cycle is 0.8 seconds. The central atrial systole averages 0.11 seconds and can rest (diastole) 0.69 seconds; the ventricular systole averages 0.27 seconds and can rest 0.53 seconds, so the heart can keep beating without getting tired, there is enough time to rest.

120. See https://kknews.cc; 健康 (health).

121. The blood pressure of the aorta is about 120/80 mmHg, the vena cava is the large vein, and its blood pressure is about 2-6 mmHg, and the pulse cannot be detected in the vena cava.

122. There are superficial veins under the skin, deep veins in the muscles, and perforator veins that connect through the muscle fascia.

123. Dr. John Campbell, *Cardiovascular System 8: Capillary, circulation and tissue fluid*, YouTube.

124. Dr. John Campbell, *Respiratory System 1: Lungs, chest wall and diaphragm*, YouTube.

125. Ibid.

126. See https://en.wikipedia.org.wiki.fractal, "fractal." The fractal or fractal pattern was first named by the mathematician Benoit Mandelbrot in 1975. It is a special set of numbers that shows similarity across the entire range—that is, they look the same no matter how big or small. Another characteristic of fractals is that they exhibit great complexity

127. Dr. John Campbell, *Respiratory System 4: Alveoli and gaseous exchange,* YouTube.

128. Dr. John Campbell, *Respiratory System 2: breathing and ventilation,* YouTube.

129. See https://en.wikipedia.org.wiki.humandigestivesystem, "*human digestive system,*"; Emma Bryce, *How your digestive system works,* YouTube, 2017; Dr. John Campbell, Digestive System, Part 1: Crash Course Anatomy & Physiology #33, YouTube.

130. Dr. John Campbell, *Digestive System, Part 1: Crash Course Anatomy & Physiology #33*, YouTube.

131. Dr. John Campbell, *Urinary System, Part 1: Crash Course Anatomy & Physiology #38,* YouTube.

132. See https://en.wikipedia.org.wiki.kidney, "kidney."

133. Paul Andersen, *The Endocrine System*, YouTube, 2012.

134. Emma Bryce, *You and Your Hormones, Society for Endocrinology,* YouTube, 2015

135. Emma Bryce, *how does your immune system work?* YouTube, 2018

136. Dr. John Campbell, *Nervous System 8: Sympathetic and parasympathetic*, YouTube.

137. See https://en.wikipedia.org.wiki.homeostasis, "homeostasis"; also Dr. John Campbell, *Homeostasis 3: Thermoregulation*, YouTube.

138. See https://en.wikipedia.org.wiki.enzyme, "enzyme."

139. Ibid.

140. See https://en.wikipedia.org.wiki.Trinity, "Trinity."

141. Ibid.

142. Jesus said: *"God is spirit, and his worshipers must worship in the Spirit and in truth"* (John 4:24).

143. See https://en.wikipedia.org.wiki.electromagnetic, "electromagnetic." The light waves of visible light are visible electromagnetic waves

144. A vector is a basic concept in natural sciences. It refers to a quantity that has both magnitude and direction. Vectors often use line length to indicate the size of the quantity and an arrow to indicate the direction to distinguish pure quantities that are only expressed by line length. The concept opposite of a vector is called a scalar or quantity, that is, there is only size and no direction. For example, speed has a direction, while distance is only a quantity.

145. *"God is love"* (1 John 4:16 NIV)

146. Chuck Missler, "The Camp of Israel," Lambert Dolphin's Place, http://www.ldolphin.org.camp, 1995.

147. See "Tent of Meeting," Dictionary of Bible Themes, 7474, https://www.biblegateway.com.resources.7474.

148. *"When he had received the drink, Jesus said, 'It is finished.' With that, he bowed his head and gave up his spirit"* (John 19:30 NIV).

149. *"Therefore, brothers and sisters, since we have confidence to enter the Most Holy Place by the blood of Jesus, by a new and living way opened for us through the curtain, that is, his body"* (Hebrews 10:19–20 NIV).

www.ingramcontent.com/pod-product-compliance
Lightning Source LLC
Chambersburg PA
CBHW051219120626
46547CB00013B/1415